PHILADELPHIA cooks ITALIAN

150+ Recipes from the former
Italian Market, Little Italy and Famous Eateries

Celeste A. Morello

PHILADELPHIA cooks ITALIAN

150+ Recipes from the former
Italian Market, Little Italy and Famous Eateries

Front cover: *top left*: unidentified Italian at northwest corner of 9th and Christian Streets, c. 1905; *top right*: Nicola Marinelli's bread truck on South 8th Street, below Kimball Street, c. 1910; *bottom left*: Pasquale Ingenito's produce wagon at 826 Christian Street, c. 1900; *bottom right*: Josephine Parisi at her store, 1154 South 9th Street, c. 1930.

No portion of this book can be used, copied or transmitted electronically except with written consent by the author.

Published in the United States of America.

ISBN: 0-9770532-2-9

Library of Congress Control Number: 2010940522

Copyright 2010.

Table Of Contents

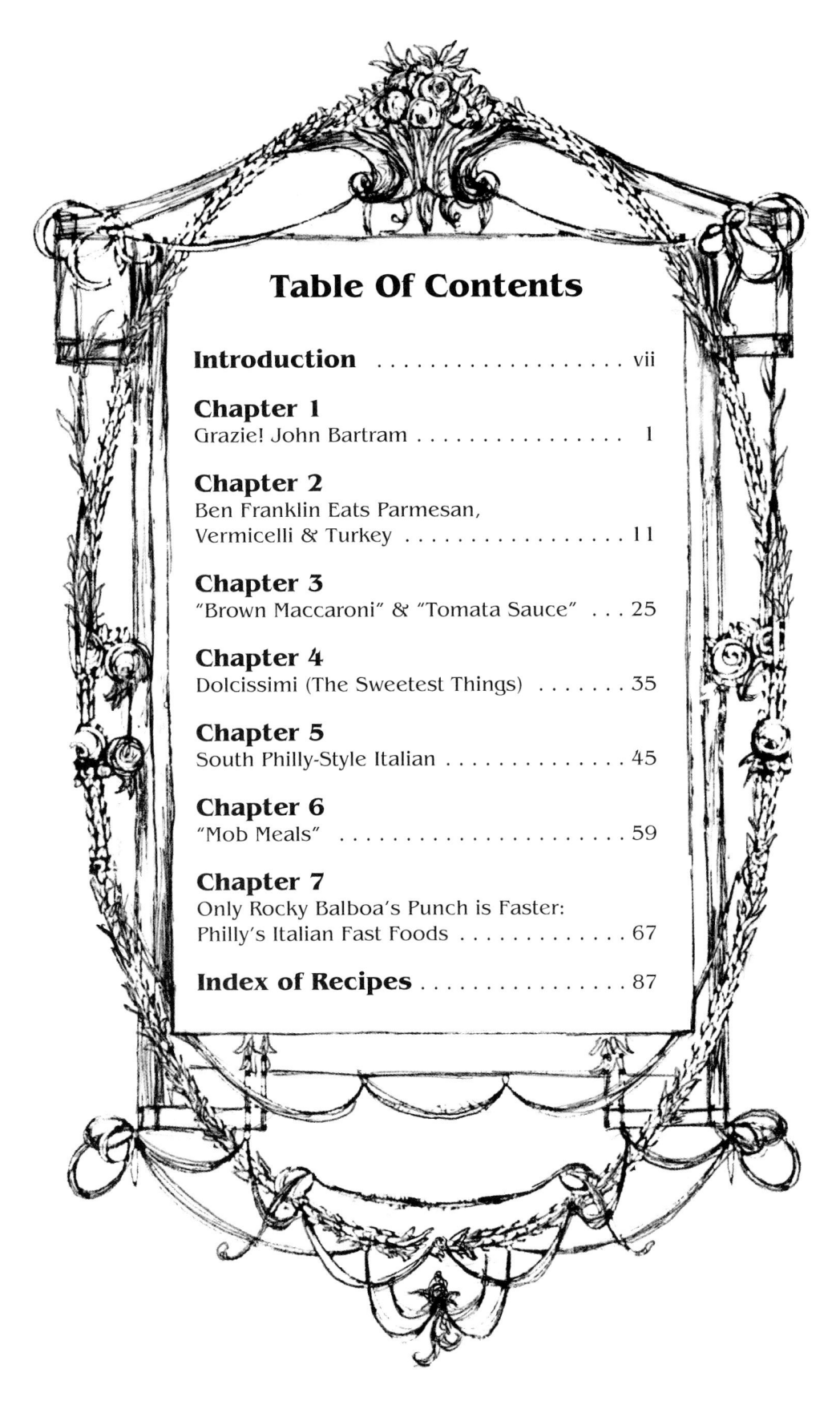

Introduction vii

Chapter 1
Grazie! John Bartram 1

Chapter 2
Ben Franklin Eats Parmesan,
Vermicelli & Turkey 11

Chapter 3
"Brown Maccaroni" & "Tomata Sauce" . . . 25

Chapter 4
Dolcissimi (The Sweetest Things) 35

Chapter 5
South Philly-Style Italian 45

Chapter 6
"Mob Meals" 59

Chapter 7
Only Rocky Balboa's Punch is Faster:
Philly's Italian Fast Foods 67

Index of Recipes 87

INTRODUCTION

Italian food is so agreeable that its origins in the United States would be of interest to almost everyone, as it is to Philadelphians who have been eating "Italian" for about three hundred years. Eating Italian depends on cooking Italian with the ease to do it fast, as well as slow to make foods taste remarkably wonderful—because Italian food is awfully good!

This book combines recipes from my cookbooks, **The Philadelphia Italian Market Cookbook** and **Philadelphia's Italian Foods** which documented the historical roots of how Italian foods were transported to this nation and what changes developed from influences already in Philadelphia's growth, trade and natural environment. I also recorded recipes from some of Philadelphia's eateries that no longer survive, such as Palumbo's, South Philly Grille, Felicia's and Cous' Little Italy, a favorite with the local mobsters.

The recipes are easy: they've already been tried for years and the responses I had received deserve their re-publication in this recipe book. So, **cuoca bene e mangia!** (Cook well and eat!)

Now, you'll enjoy how Philadelphians cook Italian and love it!

Little Italy preschoolers (here in about 1907) snack on treats supervised by acculturated Italian Americans who knew what could be made or brought into Philadelphia to eat.

CHAPTER 1
GRAZIE! John Bartram

Cooking Italian in Philadelphia begins with how Italian produce and foods were transported across the Atlantic to our fledgling town where northern Europeans settled. The Swedes who formed the first colony in Philadelphia managed on corn and grains, supplemented by game meats and fish, which the British also ate. Then, scientist John Bartram (1699-1777), who became King George III's "Royal Botanist" communicated with fellow botanists in England and Sweden and was able to plant what they sent him in his farm in Philadelphia. Produce from the Mediterranean was highly desirable—delicious and exotic—and the foods were memories of visiting the ancient lands of the Romans and Greeks of antiquity that was popular among the British elite. By 1750, colonists in Philadelphia were able to use the same herbal seasonings that cooks on the Italian peninsula had used for centuries, thanks to John Bartram: sweet basil (arrived in 1737): oregano (1761); and sweet marjoram (1741) then the winter sweet marjoram variety (1761). Garlic was a medicinal, as were other herbs that typically were grown for medieval apothecaries. But, ahhh! Bartram would have to wait to get tomato seeds for his friend, Peter Collinson had none yet in 1759.

Citrus was imported, not grown in the Philadelphia climate. The following recipes could have been eaten in Philadelphia by 1750, with the exception of olive oil as an ingredient, a loss to colonial Philadelphians' good health.

PARADISO RISTORANTE'S PAPPARDELLE con FUNGHI RAGU

1 lb. fresh pappardelle pasta, cooked, on side
1 lb. portobello mushrooms, stems off, and sliced
1 lb. shiitake mushrooms, stems off, and sliced
6 T extra virgin olive oil   6 T heavy cream
2 shallots, chopped fine   1 T fresh rosemary, chopped
1 C chicken stock or veal stock   1 C dry white wine
1 T fresh thyme, chopped fine   salt & pepper to taste

In a heavy skillet, over medium heat, pour in the oil and cook the shallots until translucent. Add the mushrooms and stir for about 5 minutes. Raise the heat to medium high and add wine. Cook until reduced, about 2 minutes. Add stock and simmer 3 to 5 minutes, gradually adding the cream. Lastly, add the seasonings. Toss over the cooked pasta. If ragu is too thick, add some water. Serves 6 as a main course, or 8 as an appetizer. Spread ragu on meats, too.

CLAIRE DiLULLO SCHIAVONE'S APPETIZER
(From "Moonstruck," formerly, "DiLullo's")

8 medium sweet peppers (use red, yellow, orange or purple)
16 flat anchovy fillets   3 T capers
4 cloves garlic, crushed   oregano leaves
extra virgin olive oil to drizzle

Roast peppers over flame til blackened, then place in paper or plastic bag to steam them. Scrape off skins, the seeds and "blackened" parts. Lay peppers in a 8" X 10" dish and put anchovy fillets on top. Sprinkle with capers, garlic and oregano. Repeat until all ingredients are gone. Cover with oil. Cut and serve. Makes 8 portions.

AUNT CONNIE IPPOLITO'S MUSSELS IN WHITE SAUCE
(From "Ippolito's Seafood")

5 lbs. white water mussels, cleaned and debearded
1 1/4 C dry white wine
1 C blended oil
1 (8 oz. jar) clam juice
1/4 C fresh Italian parsley, chopped
1 T dry basil
6-8 cloves garlic, chopped
1/3 stick butter
1 1/2 C water
salt to taste
crushed red pepper to taste

Saute garlic in oil until lightly golden. Add all ingredients into a deep pot to hold mussels. Cover and cook over medium heat shaking the pot occasionally during cooking. Steam until all mussels are fully opened, then serve 6 to 8 hungry diners.

MELOGRANO RISTORANTE'S SALAD

1 head Savoy cabbage, julienned
12 (16-20 size) shrimp, grilled
1 C creamy cheese (like a gorgonzola
2 C baby arugula
1 Granny Smith apple, julienned

Dressing: Crush or use food processor
1/4 C toasted walnuts
3 T white balsamic vinegar
pinch of white pepper
1 t Dijon mustard
3 T extra virgin olive oil

Lay greens down first then lay apples and cheese atop, garnishing with the shrimp. Pour dressing and serve.

LA LOCANDA del GIOTTONE'S ITALIAN DUCK

1 breast of duck, julienned
1/2 C flour to dust
2-3 sage leaves
1 T butter
Italian parsley

2 T extra virgin olive oil
2 cloves garlic, chopped
1/2 C white wine
1 C chicken stock
salt & pepper to taste

Saute garlic in oil and add the duck, cooking over medium heat until brown. Add remaining ingredients and simmer. This serves one breast per person, so adjust recipe to number of persons who will have this as a main course, or add one pound of pasta, toss with the breast meat and serve 4.

Alfio Casella's 1922 "Poultry Market" was no different from the first purveyors in Philadelphia: where "fresh" meats meant "freshly slaughtered" and the products were in the same wooden containers.

MAMA YOLANDA'S RESTAURANT'S LIVER CASALINGA
(The John Righi, Jr. recipe)

2 calves livers, in long strips	2 green sweet peppers, cut in strips
2 medium Spanish onions, sliced	1 C white wine
1 C any stock	1 T butter
2-3 cloves of garlic, minced	2 strips of bacon
2 T olive oil	1 T parsley
1/2 C flour	salt & pepper to taste

Flour the liver and place in saute pan with the olive oil to brown on both sides. Drain oil, add the garlic, onions and peppers and saute until golden. Then add the stock, wine, seasonings and butter. Lay the bacon on top and simmer until done. Serves one.

LITTLE ITALY TUNA

4 fillets of tuna, 1/2" thick	1/2 C olive oil for cooking
1 onion, chopped	1/2 C balsamic vinegar
salt & pepper to taste	1/2 C fresh parsley

Sauté onions in oil until golden, then add 4 T vinegar, fish and parsley and cook over low to medium heat until done. Serves 4.

ANNAMARIE MICHETTI'S WILD RICE SALAD

4 C white rice, cooked
1 C toasted almonds   1 1/2 C dried cranberries
1 C scallions, minced   1/2 C celery, finely cut
1 red bell pepper, diced   1/3 C Italian parsley, minced

Dressing:
4 T rice vinegar   4 T lemon juice
1 garlic clove, mashed to paste   1/2 C canola oil
3 T sesame oil   salt & pepper to taste

Mix all dry ingredients together. Only add dressing when about to serve—do not mix together and hold over. Makes about 10 sides.

ANTONETTA CARUSO MARANO'S BREAKFAST FOUNDER

1 lb. (4 oz. portions) fresh filleted flounder
2 large Yukon Gold (or any white) potatoes in 1/4" pieces
1 large onion, sliced into "circles"
2 T cooking oil to fry
1/2 C Italian parsley, chopped
salt & pepper to taste

In a deep skillet over medium heat, coat the pan with oil and lightly brown the potatoes and onions for a few minutes. Season. Add about 2 C water and simmer to a boil, gradually reducing heat. Lay flounder pieces on top of the potatoes and onions and cover with lid. You may season the flounder before covering. Steam will cook the fish for 5 to 7 minutes, then serve. Optional drizzle with olive oil before eating.

FLAVORED VINEGAR

4-6 oz. shallots, finely chopped   2-4 oz. slithered garlic
1 quart red wine vinegar

Add shallots and garlic into bottled vinegar and keep covered for about 3 weeks before use as a condiment.

This condiment can be used on cold or hot foods.

CHICKEN LIVERS
(From "Villa di Roma Restaurant")

1 pt. chicken livers, to fry with 4 T cooking oil and 3 medium onions, diced

Brown livers and onions, then add to skillet over medium heat:

1 C green peppers, chopped	1 C mushrooms, chopped
1/2 t garlic powder	salt & pepper to taste
3-4 oz. lightly salted butter	1/4 + red wine

Simmer everything together. Can be served to 2 portions over a macaroni or rice.

Eighteenth century Philadelphia experienced dramatic changes in trade after the War for Independence. Limited imports came to Philadelphia's shore during most of John Bartram's accumulation of seeds and cuttings from England, where travelers to Italy sent what was banned. Philip Mazzei, a friend of Ben Franklin and Thomas Jefferson needed permission to take plants from Tuscany to America in 1773, but afterwards, the open seas and freedom from Great Britain allowed more "joys" from the many kingdoms on the Italian peninsula to arrive with welcomes. Boston, Alexandria and Philadelphia, among other large populated centers, were able to serve Mediterranean-based foods in the new nation.

Here are some side dishes and entrees that would have been possible in the eighteenth century.

BARBARA MOSES' STRING BEAN SIDE

Barbara contributed this recipe to **The Philadelphia Italian Market Cookbook.** She has been an educator and high school principal in the Philadelphia School District, and a 9th Street shopper for years.

2 lbs. string beans	1 small onion, slithered
1 carrot, shaved in strips	a ham bone with some meat
salt & pepper to taste	

In a deep pot with about 2 quarts of water, place vegetables in boiling water with the ham bone and 2 T salt. Cook until beans are soft, Seasoned salt is what Barbara uses to taste. Makes 4 to 6 servings.

STEVE CANDELORO'S HONEY SALMON

Steve owns "New York Bakery" and makes an unmistakable bread. He cooks this for his family.

1 1/2 lb. salmon fillets
1 T granulated garlic
pure honey to drizzle
2 T Italian seasoning
2 T butter

"Smother" both sides of fillets with butter, then seasoning before baking in preheated oven for 5 to 7 minutes at 350°F. Remove from oven and drizzle with honey. Serves 4.

MARTINA BONUOMO GIUNTA'S VEAL ROAST

Mrs. Giunta is the daughter and wife of butchers. Her son, Charles owns "Giunta's Prime Meats" at Reading Terminal Market; another son, Martin owns "Martin's Meats" also at the Terminal.

4-5 lb. boneless veal shoulder roast
sprig of rosemary, chopped fine
  & sprig for garnish
6-8 slices prosciutto, cut thin
salt & pepper to taste
2 cloves garlic, chopped
olive oil to rub
1/4 lb. sharp provolone

Pound meat to 1 1/2" thick then rub with oil. Season with salt, pepper, rosemary and garlic. Open the veal and lay the cheese first, then the prosciutto and roll. Tie with string, then brown on stove set on high heat in a pan. Bring pan to oven to cook at 350°F for about 2 hours or more. Garnish with sprig before roasting. Serves 8 to 10.

ITALIAN SAUSAGE, PEPPERS & ONIONS

1 lb. sweet Italian sausage
3 bell peppers, in 2" strips
2 C mushrooms (optional)

1 large onion, diced
blended oil for frying

Brown sausage over high heat in skillet, then fry onions in oil until golden. Add 2 cups water and cook over medium heat, pinching sausage to release liquid inside. Add peppers while this is cooking. This should cook for about 10 to 13 minutes, depending on the meat inside the sausage. Pork or turkey Italian are good choices with their seasonings mixing with the vegetables. Makes about 4 servings as a main meal or in an Italian roll.

ITALIAN-STYLE MUSHROOM SIDE

2 lbs. porcini mushrooms,
  cut into 1" pieces
1/4 C olive oil

2 cloves, garlic, smashed
1/2 stick butter
salt & pepper to taste

Place cut mushrooms into heated oil-butter mix in saute pan and stir, seasoning to taste. As a side dish, serves 4.

ROASTED LAMB

5-6 lb. leg of lamb
1/2 C olive oil
salt & pepper to taste

3-4 cloves garlic, small pieces
1 T rosemary

Rub oil all over meat and season. Make small cuts in muscle and insert garlic pieces. Cover with rosemary and bake at 350°F for 3 hours or 1/2 hour per pound. Meat is done when it falls off bone. Serves 1/2 lb. per person or about 10.

FAVA BEAN PATTIES

1 lb. Fava beans
1/2 C onion
1/4 t hot pepper
Salt and pepper to taste

2 cloves garlic, diced
1 t coriander
1/2 t cumin
1/2 C seasoned bread crumbs

This is best done in a food processor, mixing all together. Form patties and fry with a blended olive oil. Serves 4-6 (3 oz.) portions.

LENTICCHIE ROMANI

1 lb. lentils, pre-soaked
1 large onion, diced
2 cloves garlic, diced
salt & pepper to taste

2 qts. chicken stock
2 large carrots, diced
olive oil to saute (2 T)
fresh Italian parsley

Saute onion, garlic and carrot in oil until cooked. In deep pot, boil stock and add lentils, onion, garlic and carrot. Season with salt and pepper. Cook for 45 minutes or until lentils are soft. Stock should be reduced. Parsley can be added while cooking or after. Serves 6 to 8.

MRS. MARANO'S ITALIAN SALAD DRESSING
(This is a recipe that's over 100 years old!)

2 C olive oil—use a "dressing oil"
1/4 t paprika
1 whole garlic clove, mashed
salt & pepper to taste

1/2 t sugar
1 fresh basil leaf

Place all ingredients into a large flask and let sit to infuse for at least one day before use.

Not many U.S. cities were able to import these fruits, but Philadelphia's prominence and sophisticated citizens brought the tastes of far-away lands to the ports here to be used in cakes, pies, or Italian ices.

CHAPTER 2
BEN FRANKLIN EATS PARMESAN, VERMICELLI & TURKEY

Ben Franklin was in England when on July 9, 1769 he lamented in his letter to John Bartram how he wanted a "Receipt for making Parmesan Cheese..." In 1773, Franklin sent Bartram seeds for cabbage turnips, which Giovanni Francesco Fromond gave him from Milan. Franklin was much impressed with foods from the Italian peninsula, wanting a "Vermicelli and Macaroni Maker" from Philip Mazzei's travels to Tuscany, and recommending Milanese nobility to visit Bartram's botanical garden as it was growing. (Bartram's Garden is located at 54th Street & Lindbergh Boulevard and is a National Historic Landmark House and Garden, open to the public.)

Franklin also promoted what our country had in native foods such as turkey (which he wanted to be a "national bird") and corn. Unlike when a colony of Great Britain, the United States openned trade with other countries to enable more foods from southern Europe to be on our tables. Franklin, like Jefferson, also saw the commercial value for our farmers to diversify what they grew.

Turkey has been a substitute meat for chicken recipes and the dishes that follow can have either to make what has been cooked in South Philadelphia, via central and southern Italy for decades. The recipes here are from Mrs. Marion Caltabiano whose husband, "Henry Colt" was Chubby Checkers' manager when "The Twist" became a hit. Kippee Palumbo's husband Frank made "Palumbo's" a name in entertainment and good food.

Caltabiano Poultry was sold at the 9th Street "Italian Market" and in New Jersey where turkey overshadowed chicken in trade. Here the owners, Marion & Henry (second couple from the left), and friends dine out at Palumbo's.

MARION CALTABIANO'S TURKEY SCALLOPINI

8 turkey scallops
1 clove garlic, crushed
8 sliced each: prosciutto and mozzarella
Salt and pepper to taste

2 T butter
sprig of rosemary
3 T sherry (or Marsala wine)
1/4 C chicken/turkey stock

Pound scallops between two pieces of waxed paper. Melt butter in pan over medium head and add turkey and garlic and simmer until brown on both sides. Lay ham on scallops. Add sherry, stock and rosemary. Cover and cook for 10 minutes. Place in a pan, lay cheese on top and pour liquid over, then cover to let cheese melt. Serves 4.

KIPPEE PALUMBO'S TURKEY (or CHICKEN) ROSEMARY

2 large breasts (or 4 large chicken breasts)
1 stick butter or 1/4 C oil
2 whole cooking onions

1/4 C rosemary, crushed
salt & pepper to taste

In a large baking pan, wash meats then rub on all sides with salt and pepper, then drizzle oil or melted butter onto skins. Sprinkle with rosemary and cover with foil. Put onions (or any other vegetable, like yams or sweet potatoes) in pan and bake 45 minutes covered, then 45 minutes uncovered.

Now, here's a nice side to go with the poultry:

ESCAROLE & WHITE BEANS

2 lbs. escarole
1 (15 or 16 oz. can) white beans
3 cloves garlic, chopped
Optional: hot pepper flakes

3 T olive oil
1 C chicken stock
salt & pepper to taste

Wash and blanch escarole. In a deep pan saute garlic in oil and add greens. Season. Rinse beans before adding to greens and stir. Add chicken stock and simmer for 30 minutes. Serves 4.

Ben Franklin's love of parmesan cheese is honored in these recipes from the former Italian Market neighborhood in Bella Vista and from the eateries in Philadelphia whose chefs hail from the Lombard and Tuscan areas in Italy.

BROCCOLI & MACARONI

8 T olive oil
4 cloves garlic, minced
1 C chicken broth
1 C fresh parsley, chopped
any small pasta

2 T butter
1 bunch broccoli, in florets
1 C fresh basil, chopped
1 C parmesan cheese
salt & pepper to taste

Heat oil with butter in a skillet to cook garlic with the florets. Add the broth and cover until it boils. Simmer 5-8 minutes or until broccoli is still firm, then add the basil and pasta. Liquid may evaporate, so add water to keep moist. Toss with parmesan cheese and garnish with parsley. Serves 4.

CAULIFLOWER PARMESAN

1 head, cauliflower
1/2 C parmesan cheese (or more)
Seasoned Italian bread crumbs
1 C parsley, chopped

2 eggs, beaten
1 C flour
salt & pepper

Break cauliflower into small pieces, then dip into egg with the cheese, parsley and seasonings. Then dip into flour, then again in the egg, then in the bread crumbs. Fry in blended olive oil until golden. Pat dry on a paper towel. Toss with parmesan cheese so the vegetable is coated before serving. Makes about 4 sides.

PARMESAN BEANS

1 lb. string beans or snow peas
2 cloves, garlic, minced
blended olive oil for frying
1/2 C parmesan cheese
Italian bread crumbs
salt & pepper to taste

Heat skillet with oil for garlic to cook, then add the beans/peas and season. Add water or broth to cook vegetables for 3-5 minutes. Toss the cooked vegetables with the parmesan and bread crumbs. Serves 4.

SPALAGI a la SALVATRICE
(As prepared for "Ristorante Panorama")

1 bunch, asparagus
1/2 lb. prosciutto
2 cloves garlic, chopped
1 C (or more) roasted peppers
1 C shredded parmesan cheese
2 T capers
2 T parsley, chopped
1/2 C olive oil
juice of one lemon

Grill asparagus on a rack for about 5 minutes, then wrap prosciutto around 6 stalks. Place on a dish. In a bowl, mix capers, garlic, oil, lemon and parsley and pour over asparagus. Top with shredded parmesan and roasted peppers. Serves 3 (2 per person).

SOUTH PHILLY-STYLE CHEESE FILLING

To use in ravioli, lasagna or manicotti. In a large bowl, combine:

2 lbs. ricotta cheese
8 oz. mozzarella, shredded
pinch pepper
3 T Italian parsley, chopped fine
1/3 C parmesan, grated
2 eggs
1 t salt

Yields enough for a 9" X 12" lasagna dish with two layers.

Claudio Auriemma (1935 – 1991) peers out from the products used by all of the chefs in the 5-star and Mobile Guide–rated restaurants in the Philadelphia region. "Claudio's King of Cheese" is the largest Italian specialty food emporium in the Delaware Valley Area.

Do not be intimidated by these Milanese dishes—they will impress those who will eat them and not realize how easy they are to do.

FRESCA PASTA LOMBARDA

1 lb. medium-cut cooked pasta
1 C artichoke hearts
1/4 C Italian parsley, chopped
1/2 C parmesan (grated)
1/4 C extra virgin olive oil
1/2 C roasted peppers, diced
1/2 C any green olive, cut
1 C fresh spinach, chopped
1/2 C red wine vinegar
salt & pepper to taste

Combine all ingredients after cutting into bite-sized pieces to mix with the cooked macaroni. Serves 4 to 6 as an entree.

MARCO AVIGO'S RISOTTO LOMBARDO

8 oz. arborio rice
1 T onion, minced
1 T butter
2 T extra virgin olive oil
1 T parmesan cheese
1/2 bag, saffron
1/2 glass white wine
1 C vegetable stock
6 jumbo shrimp
1 small zucchini, cubed
1/2 clove garlic, smashed

In a skillet over medium heat saute the onion with butter and oil until golden, then add the rice and stir in the wine. Boil to reduce over the next 15 to 18 minutes. On the side, dissolve the saffron in the cup of vegetable stock, then add to the rice. Cook for 5 minutes more, then turn off heat. Aside, steam the shrimp, then cut into bite-sized pieces. Saute the zucchini in oil and garlic and add the shrimp, stir, then add to rice mix with butter, parmesan and seasonings. Serves 2.

BONZETTA
(Stuffed Veal)

1/2 lb. breast of veal	2 strips bacon
1/2 C onions, diced	1/2 C diced celery
1/4 C Italian parsley	2-3 C fresh bread
1/2 C parmesan cheese	4-5 eggs beaten
8 oz. swiss chard, chopped	salt & pepper to taste

In a skillet, cook the onions, celery, parsley and bacon until done. Add sauteed mix to a bowl with the bread broken in small pieces. Add eggs and mix together with the greens. Stuff in a veal pocket that already had salt & pepper in cavity. Cook at 350°F in oven for about 2 hours. Serves 4 to 6.

MARCO AVIGO'S SAUSAGE & BROCCOLI RABE
(Formerly served in "Sfizzio")

1 lb. pork sausage	2 bunches, broccoli rabe, washed
3 T olive oil for frying	3 cloves garlic, chopped finely
hot pepper flakes to taste	salt & pepper to taste

Heat a skillet filled with water to cook the vegetable through until it is tender, then drain the water, add oil and saute the garlic with the greens over medium heat. Season to taste. Add the sausage and continue to simmer to let the sausage's flavors infuse the greens. Cook this slow. Serves 3 to 4.

THE SALOON'S LIVORNAISE SAUCE

2 stalks celery	1/2 carrot
1/2 onion	

Mash these together in a food processor until grainy. Drain liquid. In a skillet over medium heat, combine:

1 anchovy	3 T extra virgin olive oil
1/4 t flour	1 T butter
8 oz. white wine	2 T marinara sauce
2 sprigs thyme	1 bay leaf

First make a roux with the flour and butter, then add remaining ingredients, along with the first mixed blend. Stir together. This is used atop fish, mostly, but can be spread atop meat. This is a portion for one serving.

SCANNICCHIO'S RESTAURANT'S VEAL MILANESE
(Recipe prepared for Frank Sinatra)

12 oz. veal chop, split to butterfly and pounded thin
3 T blended oil, or olive oil
1/2 C pecorino romano cheese
1 C Italian seasoned bread crumbs
3 sprigs Italian parsley, chopped
3 eggs, whisked, set aside
salt & pepper to taste

In a bowl, beat the eggs, then add salt and pepper, cheese, parsley and mix together. Dredge the veal in the egg mix, coat with breadcrumbs and pan fry over medium heat in the olive oil on both sides. Place skillet in a preheated oven set at 225°F for 10 minutes.

Sinatra salad to go with veal chop:
1 C baby arugula
8 grape tomatoes, sliced once
extra virgin olive oil
lemon cut to squeeze
1/2 lb. small mozzarella balls
1 t capers
balsamic "to splash"
salt & pepper to taste

Serve this dish by laying the veal on a plate with the salad on top. Serves 2.

Philip Mazzei, a native of Florence, Italy had written: "All men are by nature equally free and independent...equal to each other in natural rights" which impressed Thomas Jefferson who paraphrased this as "All men are created free and equal" in the Declaration of Independence—written in Philadelphia at 7th and Market Streets. Mazzei's Florentine diet also inspired our Franklin and Jefferson, and chefs from Tuscany still cook in the city the same dishes as would have been eaten by 18th century Philadelphians. Here are some:

LaBUCA'S GNOCCHI a la FIORENTINE
(by Tuscan Giuseppe Giuliani)

2 C spinach
2 eggs
1 1/2 C parmesan cheese
flour for dusting
1 1/2 C ricotta cheese
pinch of nutmeg
1 C butter
salt & pepper to taste

Cook and drain spinach, then add the ricotta and mix. Add eggs, nutmeg, salt and pepper, then add the parmesan and re-mix. Refrigerate.

In a mixing bowl, line with flour. Roll the cold spinach mix into little balls about 1/2" and coat each ball with the flour, then roll again so the flour covers the ball. Preheat a pot with salted water to boil and gently add the balls to the boiling water until they float to the top. Remove with a skimmer and place in a bowl to cover. Moisten with softened butter and turn. Sprinkle parmesan generously and serve as a main course or side for 4.

Another version of gnocchi:

MARIE MIGLINO'S RICOTTA GNOCCHI
(from "Felicia's Restaurant")

1 lb. whole milk ricotta
1/2 t salt
1 egg
1 1/2 C flour

Mix ingredients in a large bowl until consistent, then place a handful upon a floured surface and roll out into a rope about 1/2" thick. Cut into 1" pieces and place in boiling, salted water for 2-3 minutes. Remove and serve with sauce. Serves 4 to 6.

VEAL FLORENTINE
(From "Marra's Cucina Italiana")

1/2 C olive oil
3 veal medallions (4 oz. each)
3 cloves garlic, chopped
1 C mushrooms
1/2 C dry Marsala wine
1/2 C veal stock
1/2 C flour "to dust"
1 T butter
2 C fresh or frozen spinach
1 slice prosciutto
1 slice mozzarella

Dust each medallion, then place in skillet with oil on medium heat. Cook for 2 minutes on each side, then saute garlic until golden. Add mushrooms, stirring constantly. Add wine, stock and butter. Remove from heat. Warm spinach in separate saucepan, draining off water. Plate the veal and top with spinach, then with the prosciutto and mozzarella. Heat this plate in oven until cheese melts. This is for 2 servings.

JOHN & MARIE LaTERZA'S "JUMBOT"
(A Vegetarian's Dream!)

5 medium potatoes
2 each: red, green & yellow peppers, sliced
1 medium onion, chopped
3 tomatoes, chopped
salt & pepper to taste

2 large eggplants (or zucchini)
3 t dried basil

2 T olive oil
5 cloves garlic, minced
1 lb. mushrooms, sliced

Cut peeled potatoes and eggplants and set aside. In dutch oven, saute onion and garlic in oil until golden over medium heat, then add peppers and cook until half done. Add eggplant, mushrooms and tomatoes. Season. Simmer with lid on until potatoes are soft. Serves 6 to 8 with some crusty Italian bread to soak juices.

Before 1850, Philadelphians had the ingredients to make these dishes because the port brought in citrus and the Jersey and Maryland coastlines made seafood a local delight for all.

Who could forget "Palumbo's" crab cakes (if you are of an age to remember one of the city's favorite Italian restaurants!)

ROBERT DONATO'S CRAB CAKES
(From "Palumbo's")

4 lbs. lump crab meat
1/2 C Italian parsley, chopped
1 Spanish onion, diced
3 cloves garlic, finely chopped
4 T extra virgin olive oil
1/4 T "Old Bay" seasoning

1 stalk celery, diced
1 lb. butter
3/4 C flour
1 qt. heavy cream
1/3 t paprika
1 shot glass of sherry

Saute onions and garlic in oil, then add celery. In saucepan, make a roux of butter and flour, then slowly add cream over medium heat, stirring constantly. Add seasonings and parsley, then fold in crab meat and sherry. Lastly, add sauteed onions and garlic. Bake in oven for 20 minutes at 350°F, or roll in flour, then in beaten eggs, then in breadcrumbs and fry in vegetable oil until browned. Yield is 8 crab cakes at 8 oz. each.

Souvenir Photo
PALUMBO'S
SINCE 1884

Celebrations at "Palumbo's" were often photographed, as this album cover suggests, to remember good times at one of the few places in Philadelphia where crowds of up to 700 could gather. "Palumbo's" began as a boarding house in 1884, as did "Dante & Luigi's" Restaurant in 1899.

CLAMS & SPAGHETTI
(From "Dante & Luigi's Restaurant")

1 lb. spaghetti, cooked on side
3 T olive oil
1 1/2 T fresh onion, minced
1/3 C white wine
1 C fresh fish stock
salt & pepper to taste

48 little neck clams in shells
1 1/2 T garlic, sliced
2 oz. fresh basil
1 qt. marinara sauce
"touch" red pepper flakes

In skillet over medium heat saute garlic and onion in oil until golden. Season, then add clams and stir. Pour in wine until it is reduced. Add stock and simmer 3 minutes before pouring marinara and seasonings. Cook 3 to 6 minutes until clams open, then spoon clams and sauce over pasta. Serves 2 to 4.

SICILIAN BLOOD ORANGE SALAD

5-6 blood oranges, peeled & halved
1 C black olives, pitted
1/2 C red onion, diced
salt to taste
1/4 C extra virgin olive oil
6 anchovies, cut in half
1 T course ground pepper

Combine all ingredients and serve promptly. Makes 4-6 portions

JIM TROVARELLO'S SEAFOOD SALAD

A former Federal agent, Jim's ancestors arrived in Philadelphia through Antonio Palumbo, who laid the foundation for "Palumbo's" cafe and nightclub from what had been a boarding house for the Italian immigrants he brokered abroad for city jobs.

2 dozen medium shrimp, shelled and cubed
1 lb. fresh cod fillets   1/2 C picante pepper, diced
olive oil to drizzle

Preheat oven to 350°F. In a pyrex baking dish, broil cod until it flakes then remove it from the oven. Add shrimp, pepper and drizzle with oil, tossing lightly while still warm. Serves 2-3.

"DiNARDO'S FAMOUS CRABS'" CRAB SOUP
(Compliments of Liz Massimo, the Owner)

8 oz. frozen peas & carrots
12 oz. frozen string beans
1/4 t cayenne pepper
1/2 onion, diced
1/4 head cabbage, diced
8 oz. can tomato puree
8 oz. crab meat
8 oz. frozen lima beans
2 T butter
3 T "Old Bay" seasoning
2 stalks celery, diced
8 oz. can crushed tomatoes
1 T crab base

Place all ingredients, except the crab meat, in a soup pot to boil over high heat. The pot should hold about 4 quarts of water. Simmer for 20 minutes on medium to low heat. Add crab while it simmers.

Serves 6 to 8.

FISH & LEMONS

4 (4.oz.) pieces of flounder, halibut, cod or any cold water fish, filleted
extra virgin olive oil

1 C chicken broth
2 lemons, thinly sliced
salt & pepper to taste

Pour broth into pan and lay lemons atop each fish piece. Season. Broil in oven set at 350°F for 5 to 8 minutes until lemons cook. Drizzle with oil before serving. Makes 4 entrees.

Little Italy civic leader and pasta entrepreneur Antonio Raggio migrated from Genoa, Italy to Philadelphia in 1855.

The southern Italians who settled in the city during The Great Migration (1890-1920) formed his customer base for locally-made dry macaroni.

CHAPTER 3
"BROWN MACCARONI" & "TOMATA SAUCE"

By the 1840s, Philadelphians were integrating more Italian foods into daily cooking with stores that sold "vermicelli" and the generic "maccaroni" that was smaller and bite-sized for soups and sides. The "maccaroni" was imported and brown because the flour was unbleached. Cookbooks printed in the city noted that "tomatas" were better accepted than before as edible—not poisonous as its previous reputation had. But the marriage of macaroni in tomato sauce was still afar, leaving "tomata sauce" to be used more as a condiment. "Stewed tomatas" was a side vegetable (or is it a fruit?) and was an ingredient in soups, stews, pies and in roasts.

Dr. Richard Juliani from Villanova University specialized in Philadelphia's first Italians and wrote extensively on the settlement begun by Genoese immigrants in the 1830s and 1840s in what is now South Philadelphia, formerly the "Little Italy" of the past.

The Philadelphia Italian Market Cookbook captured some of the dishes made by the Genoese from their descendants, reproduced here:

BISHOP JAMES SCHAD'S SKIRT STEAK

4 (4 oz.) steaks 1/2" thick
1/2 C seasoned bread crumbs
1 egg

1 (16 oz.can) spinach
1/3 C locatelli cheese, grated
salt & pepper to taste

Pound the steaks thin and season. In a bowl, mix spinach, egg, breadcrumbs and cheese and fill each steak with some stuffing. Tie each steak with twine to make four bundles. Bake in oven at 350°F and turn occasionally for about 10 minutes. Serves 4.

RISTORANTE ILLUMINARE'S PESTO SAUCE

1 bunch basil
2 T pine nuts
2 T walnuts
2 garlic cloves

1/2 C any cooking oil
3 T parmesan cheese
3 T pecorino romano cheese
salt & pepper to taste

This is for a food processor and is a small batch: blend until smooth, adding oil last. Makes 1 to 2 cups.

TRADITIONAL PESTO SAUCE
(For those who want extra virgin olive oil)

2 C basil
1/4 C pinuola nuts
1/2 C parmesan cheese
warm water or heavy cream

2 cloves, garlic
1 C extra virgin olive oil
fresh ground black pepper (opt.)
salt to taste

Add more cheese or basil to one's liking, but prepare all in a food processor for better consistency. Makes 3-4 C pesto.

CAPER SAUCE

1 stick butter

1 T capers
1 T red wine vinegar

3 T (or more) Italian parsley, minced
1/2 t salt

Cook this over medium heat in a saucepan. Pour over fish or a vegetable like broccoli or cauliflower.

MUSSELS GENOVESE

2 doz. mussels, debearded and cleaned
2 qts. prepared marinara sauce   basil leaves
2 T olive oil   1 C heavy cream
salt & pepper to taste

In a deep pot, warm the marinara sauce over medium heat, adding some water to thin the sauce. Add mussels and cover to steam until mussels are opened. Add cream to tomato sauce, basil leaves and seasonings. Simmer 3 to 5 minutes until flavors blend. Serves about 2.

Founded in 1880, Raggio and Guano's macaroni factory was said to be one of the first in the U.S. Located at Seventh and Montrose Streets, 54 workers posed for this photograph in about 1905.

LIGURIAN-STYLE RAVIOLI FILLING

This can be used inside the ravioli, in shells, or in lasagna.

1 lb. spinach	3 T olive oil
1 lb. ground veal, or the traditional meat: calves' brains and organ meats	2 eggs, beaten
	2 T parsley, chopped
	1 medium onion, chopped
salt & pepper to taste	2 oz. parmesan cheese

In a skillet, saute the onion until golden, then add the veal, spinach and cook until meat is done. Cool. In a bowl, place the meat mix with the greens and blend in the eggs, cheese and seasonings. One pound of lasagna or more should suffice; filling for about 16 ravioli, or for about 4 servings.

BECHAMEL SAUCE
(By Rick DeStefano at "The Victor Cafe")

1 large onion, minced	1 T unsalted butter
1/2 C sherry	2 qts. heavy cream
1 t nutmeg, freshly grated	the roux: 4 T butter
	4 T flour

In a saucepan over low heat, whisk slowly the flour and butter to form the roux. In another saucepan over medium heat, cook onions in butter until the onions are clear, then add the sherry and stir until sherry is reduced. Add the heavy cream and raise heat to a boil to simmer. Sauce should get very thick. Add the roux and nutmeg while lowering the heat, constantly stirring. Use this sauce over pastas and meats.

D'MEDICI RISTORANTE'S STUFFED STEAK

2 lbs. whole steak, butterflied
1 C olive oil
4 cloves garlic, minced
salt & pepper to taste

2 C beef stock
4 carrots, sliced
2 onions, sliced

Stuffing:
1 1/2 bags bread stuffing
2 C parmesan cheese
salt & pepper

6 eggs
1 pt. chicken stock
1/2 C Italian parsley, chopped

Brown outside and inside of steak at 500°F in the oven. On stove mix stuffing ingredients together. Marinate the steak in the roasting pan with the oil, garlic and seasonings inside and out, then stuff. Cook the onions and carrot pieces with the stock in the roasting pan with the steak and bake for 30-40 minutes at 325°F. Serves 4.

Immigrants from Rome, Italy also arrived in Philadelphia with the political turmoil abroad, becoming members of the first Italian Catholic parish in the United States, St. Mary Magdalen di Pazzi Church, founded in 1852 with the assistance of St. John Neumann. Recipes cooked in Rome could also have been made in Philadelphia at that time, with local purveyors providing the fish, meats and ingredients to be authentically "Italian."

SHRIMP & BEANS
(From "La Buca Restaurant")

1 lb. small shrimp (4–50 ct.), cooked
1 lb. cannellini beans (previously soaked and rinsed)
1 C celery hearts, cut into cubes
4 plum tomatoes, in cubes   extra virgin olive oil
handful of fresh basil, chopped   salt & pepper to taste

Mix all ingredients together and drizzle with olive oil and seasonings. Makes about 10 portions.

POPANO al CARTOCCIO
(From "Ristorante La Veranda")

1 Popano fish weighing about 1 lb. and gutted

1/2 C cherry tomatoes, sliced in half
4-5 slices of Spanish onion   4 basil leaves
1 C white Chardonnay wine
1/2 lime—for its juice   extra virgin olive oil

Combine all ingredients and place in an aluminum foil "tent" casing that is air-tight. Place into oven at 200°F for 20-25 minutes or when "tent" inflates. Serves 1-2.

VEGETABLE MEDLEY

1 C fava beans   1 can(16 oz.) cannelloni beans
1 C asparagus tips   1/2 C baby peas
2 T extra virgin olive oil   2 cloves, garlic, minced
salt & pepper to taste

Saute garlic in hot oil until golden, then add fava beans and cook until tender. Add remaining ingredients. A creamy sauce will develop from the water and beans. Season to taste. Serves 4-6.

BISTRO ROMANO'S PASTA e FAGIOLI
(Macaroni and Beans)

8 cloves garlic, chopped   1 oz. fresh parsley
2 cans cannellini beans   1 oz. marjoram
3 stalks celery, chopped   1 oz. oregano
1 white onion, chopped   1 oz. thyme
3 qts. Stock   1/4 lb. pancetta (or bacon)
3 T olive oil   chopped into small pieces
1/4 lb. small pasta   salt & pepper to taste

Saute the garlic in a small pan over medium heat and add the fresh herbs with the oil and garlic. Add pancetta and cook for about 5 minutes over medium heat, then set aside the meat and drippings. In another pot, cook macaroni as directed and drain. In a large, deep pot, heat the stock to a boil, add the beans, celery, chopped onion and stir for about one hour, then add the sauteed herbs and pancetta to the stock. Skim the surface, if necessary. Turn off heat and let rest. Then strain the stock and remove 1/2 the vegetables and bean mixture to puree it. Add the pureed half to the original and boil for another 10 minutes. Season to taste. Add the cooked pasta at the end. Serves 6 to 8.

Parmesan cheese on top is optional.

IL PORTICO RISTORANTE'S RISOTTO con QUAGLIE
(Rice with Quail*)

2 boneless quails
1 C arborio rice
2 C white wine
3 cloves garlic, chopped
1/4 C parmesan cheese

2 C chicken stock
1 small onion, diced
1 C olive oil
1 sprig rosemary
salt & pepper to taste

Use a small skillet pan to place the quails, garlic, oil, rosemary, and seasonings into a preheated oven at 400° F for 15 minutes. Turn over and put aside. In another skillet put 3/4 C oil and brown onions for about 3 minutes on medium heat before adding rice to cook for additional 3 minutes. Add wine, 2 C water or chicken stock and seasonings to taste and simmer for 20 minutes on lowheat, stirring. Add the cheese at end of cooking time. Serves two with the quails.

*Chicken, duck or turkey can also be used.

In **Philadelphia's Italian Foods,** I traced the history of tomato sauce use from the "Stewed Tomatas" and "Baked Tomatas" evolving into "Sauce" where the cook was instructed to "Press the hole (tomata) through a hair-sieve" in the 1840s. Italian immigrants from Naples made the tomato sauce the most popular in the East Coast cities, particularly here in Philadelphia where Lancaster County farmers had been growing tomatoes before 1800. A number of tomato sauces are provided here ranging from a pomodoro, to Neapolitan-style, to Evelyn Perri's "South Philly Gravy" to The Saloon's "Putanesca" by Chuckie Palumbo. And they are all easy to prepare.

SALLY AURIEMMA'S "BASIC TOMATO SAUCE"
(From "Claudio's King of Cheese")

2 qts. canned plum tomatoes
1 C fresh basil leaves
6 whole fresh garlic cloves
salt & pepper to taste

Mrs. Auriemma said to combine all ingredients together in a large pan and cook over low to medium heat for 1/2 hour to one hour. This can be used on any pasta or dish.

THE SALOON'S PUTANESCA SAUCE
(by Chuckie Palumbo, Master Chef)

1/2 C onion, minced
1 c white wine
1/2 raw red pepper, cut in cubes
2T extra virgin olive oil
1/4 C black pitted olives
2 sprigs fresh thyme
1 clove garlic, minced
2 anchovies, chopped
1/2 hot pepper flakes
1/2 C capers
3 C prepared marinara sauce
2 basil leave

Saute onions and garlic in oil, adding anchovies. Cook until anchovies disappear. Add peppers and stir over medium heat, pouring in white wine. Add olives and capers, then pour marinara and bring to a boil so liquid evaporates. Lastly add herbs. To use over two plates.

EVELYN PERRI'S "SOUTH PHILLY GRAVY"
(From "Shank's")

1/2 C olive oil	3-4 cloves garlic, diced
1 C fresh Italian parsley	2-3 basil leaves
1 lg. can Italian plum tomatoes	2 sm. cans tomato paste
1/2 to 3/4 C romano cheese, grated	salt & pepper to taste

Meats for the gravy:
4 (4 oz.) slices bracciolo steak	fresh garlic
1 piece veal	parsley
cheese	

In a Dutch oven pot, saute garlic in oil, then add parsley and basil. Add meats to brown on all sides. Use medium heat. Add plum tomatoes and paste, rinsing out the cans with water and putting water into pot. Bring to boil for about 15 minutes, then lower the heat. Add seasonings and cheese, continuing to stir to simmer for 1 to 2 hours over low to medium heat. Sauce should thicken. Mrs. Perri adds her meatballs to this gravy also to infuse with their flavors.

THE MIGLINO'S MARINARA NAPOLITANA
(From "Felicia's Ristorante")

12-14 ripe plum tomatoes	2 cloves garlic
3 or 4 basil leaves	6 T olive oil
2 oz. parmesan, grated	salt & pepper to taste

Blanch the skins and seed the tomatoes. Heat the olive oil and add two minced garlic cloves and cook until golden. Add tomatoes and cover with lid for 15 to 20 minutes. Season. Chop basil and add to sauce. Let the sauce sit for 10 minutes, then combine it with your pasta. Add the cheese and serve.

JIM CAMPENELLA'S POMODORO SAUCE

1/2 C olive oil
1 garlic clove, crushed
1 T sugar
1 t basil leaves, dried
1 t oregano leaves, dried
1 (2 lb., 3 oz) can Italian tomatoes, undrained
1 1/2 C onion, chopped
1 (8 oz. can) tomato paste
2 T parsley, chopped
1 T salt
1/4 T (pinch) black pepper

In a Dutch oven pot, heat oil then add onions and garlic and saute. Add rest of sauce's ingredients and 1 1/2 C water, mashing the tomatoes in the pot. Bring to a boil, then reduce the heat. Simmer. Stir continually for about an hour. This is a large batch that can be used on more than 2 lbs. pasta.

BOLOGNESE SAUCE
(From "Palumbo's Nostalgia")

3 T olive oil
2 cloves, garlic, diced
1 t sugar
1 green pepper, diced
1 small onion, diced
1 (16 oz. can) crushed tomatoes
3 lbs. pork, veal & beef, chopped
1 T each: basil, oregano and Italian seasoning
1 (8 oz. can) salsa
16 oz. water

Over medium heat, saute onion and garlic in a deep pot until golden. Add remaining ingredients and stir until meat is cooked through. Add tomatoes, salsa and water to simmer for about 1 hour over low heat. Continue to stir while cooking, then it's ready to use.

CHAPTER 4

DOLCISSIMI (The Sweetest Things)

Dolly Madison was first known as Mrs. John Todd at 343 Walnut Street before she became a widow and married James Madison. They lived at 429 Spruce Street during George Washington's term as president, but it is not known if this is where Mrs. Madison first was introduced to ice cream and to the other sweets that living in the capital city exposed her to. This chapter is all on Italian American repasts—dessert items—cakes, ices, cookies, candies and whatever sugar would form to make smiles.

TIRAMISU
(From "Bistro Romano")

12 eggs whites	4 oz. powdered sugar
2 lbs. mascarpone cheese	2 oz. coffee liqueur
1 qt. coffee	3 bags ladyfingers
1 C cocoa powder	store-bought

In a deep bowl, beat eggs whites until peaks form, then slowly blend in the sugar and cheese. Set aside. In another bowl, blend coffee and liqueur together then dip each ladyfinger into this mixture. Use a 10" X 12" pan to lay each soaked cake onto the bottom, side-by-side with each touching. Spread cheese mix over cakes. Sprinkle some cocoa powder on top. Repeat with another layer of cakes, then cheese mix, then cocoa, until gone. Chill for about 4 hours before serving. For 12 portions.

LA DITTA
D. VINCENTI
910 Christian Street

Panettoni di Milano – Panforti di Siena – Mostarda di Cremona – Torroni – Gianduiotti – Cioccolattini – Frutta Candita – Caramelle di Torino – Amaretti di Saronno

PIETRO D'ABBRACCIO'S COFFEE GELATO
(From "Cafe Toscano" & "Mezzaluna")

Pietro (Peter) makes about 50 different gelato—this is easy!

4 eggs yolks	1 C milk at room temperature
4 C espresso, already made	1 C heavy cream (chilled)
8 oz. sugar	pinch of salt

With a mixer on slow speed, beat eggs and sugar together for about 5 minutes, then slowly add the milk. Add pinch of salt and keep stirring. Transfer mix to a double-boiler and on medium heat, stir for about 8 minutes until a custard is formed.

Cover and chill in refrigerator after adding the espresso. Whip the heavy cream to soft peaks, then stir into the chilled custard. A gelato-maker can finish the process and freeze the custard, but one can just place the custard in the freezer and occasionally stir the custard before serving. Makes about 8 to 12 servings.

SENATOR BUDDY CIANFRANI'S CUP CUSTARD

3 eggs	3 C milk
3/4 C sugar	1 oz. brandy
cinnamon & nutmeg	

In a large bowl, blend the eggs, milk, sugar and brandy, then place mixture in a container to put into a pan with water. Top with the spices. Preheat oven to 350°F and bake for 1 hour or more. Remove from oven and cook in refrigerator until ready to serve.

TESSIE D'ORAZIO'S RICOTTA PIE
(From "D'Orazio Foods")

Cream filling:
1 qt. milk
1 C sugar
2-3 cinnamon sticks
8 egg yolks
1/2 C corn starch
zest of one lemon

Cheese filling:
1 1/4 lbs ricotta
1 C sugar
6 eggs

In a bowl, cream eggs and sugar, then fold in ricotta. In 2-3 quart saucepan over medium heat, cook milk, eggs, sugar and corn starch. Stir constantly, then add lemon zest and cinnamon sticks. Remove sticks when thickened. Line pan with graham cracker or cook crust and put in batter. Bake at 325°F for one hour. Serve when cooled.

"ERNESTO'S 1521 CAFE'S" MUGLIACCI

This is a pudding.
1 lb. farina (use "Cream of Wheat")
2 qts. water
1 t salt
4 T butter
6 eggs
1 1/4 C sugar
2 C raisins
cinnamon to garnish

Boil water with salt and gradually add farina, stirring over low heat. Add butter and cool. Add remaining ingredients except cinnamon. Pour into a 10" X 14" greased pyrex baking dish, sprinkle with cinnamon and bake in preheated oven at 375°F for 30 to 45 minutes. Let cool before serving. Serves about 4.

JOE DiGIRONIMO'S PANNA COTTA
(From "JNA Culinary Institute")

1 C whole milk
3 C heavy cream
8 ripe figs
pinch of salt
Frangelico liqueur

2 1/2 t gelatin
6 T granulated sugar
1 piece vanilla bean or
2 t vanilla extract

In a saucepan, pour milk and add gelatin, stir. Place ice cubes and water in a deep pan and set aside. Pour heavy cream into bowl, and add vanilla—set aside. Heat milk and gelatin to a boil, stirring until gelatin is dissolved. Register temperature at 135°F. Remove from heat, then add sugar and salt. Stir. Slowly add cream and vanilla into milk mix, pour everything into a bowl and set the bowl into the "ice bath" pan. Keep stirring until thick. Distribute the panna cotta into wine glasses or ramekins and cover with plastic wrap. Refrigerate for about 4 hours. While panna is chilling, soak figs in liqueur for about 1 hour then top each panna serving with the figs and liqueur. Serves about 4.

LOU CARANGI'S ITALIAN RAISIN BREAD
(From "Carangi's Bakery")

3 oz. fresh yeast from a block
12 oz. stone ground flour
1 1/2 oz. sea salt

9 oz. water, at room temp
2 oz. natural honey
2 C raisins

Mix all ingredients together and let dough rise for 2 hours. Preheat oven for 475°F and bake the two(2) loaves for about 25 minutes or until golden brown. Makes two loaves.

L. ARATA,

IMPORTER, WHOLESALE AND RETAIL DEALER IN

FOREIGN and DOMESTIC

Fruits, Nuts, and Confectionery

612 CHESTNUT STREET,

☞ Goods delivered to all parts of the City.   PHILADELPHIA

An 1879 advertisement.

DR. ANTHONY LoBIANCO'S ITALIAN CREAM FILLING
(From "LoBianco's Bakery")

Vanilla Cream:
Bring to a boil:

2 qts. Whole milk	1 qt. water

In a separate bowl, mix:

6 C sugar	4 C flour
5 Egg yolks	1/2 C vanilla extract

Slowly add above ingredients to milk-water pot and stir over medium to high heat until a boil. Remove from heat, keep stirring and let cool.

For richer, thicker filling: Add 1 lb. ricotta.
For chocolate filling: Add 3 C unsweetened cocoa and stir.

Recipe makes one dozen cannoli fillings.

BASIC ITALIAN COOKIE DOUGH

3 1/2 C all-purpose flour
1 t baking soda
1 C sugar
pinch of salt

2 eggs
1 stick butter or margarine
1 t vanilla extract
1 t almond extract

Cream sugar with butter first, then gradually add the other ingredients to form a soft dough. Chill dough for about 3 hours before using with chocolate chips, nuts or other additions.

Bake at 350°F in oven for 10-12 minutes if cookies are spoon-sized, dropped onto greased pan. Longer time if larger cookies.

LaTERZA FAMILY ITALIAN WEDDING COOKIES

6 large eggs, lightly beaten
1 C oil
6 t baking powder

1 C sugar
1 t vanilla extract
4 C flour

On table, make a "well" with 2 C flour and add ingredients gradually forming dough and mixing. Drop teaspoonfuls of the dough onto a greased, flat pan leaving about 2" space between cookies. Bake at 350°F for 10 minutes or until edges are browning. Let cool.

ITALIAN SPONGE CAKE

4 C self-rising flour
8 eggs
2 sticks butter or margarine
3 t baking powder
1 1/2 C sugar
2 t vanilla

Cream the sugar with butter, then gradually add other ingredients and mix to consistency. Pour into greased and floured cake pan and bake in preheated oven at 350°F for 30 to 40 minutes or until knife comes out clean after inserted.

Artificial rum flavoring can be used as well as almond extract. This can also be used to make a Sicilian cassata.

AUNT STELLA'S RICOTTA CAKE

2 1/2 lbs. ricotta cheese
1 C sugar
1 t vanilla extract
16 oz. sour cream
6 eggs
6 T flour
16 oz. cream cheese

Preheat oven to 350°F. Mix all ingredients in bowl, then place in a greased and floured spring pan or Bundt-type pan. Bake for 45 minutes to 1 hour or until cake's top is cracked. Cool. This tastes better after one day.

ITALIAN LEMON ICE
(Called "Water Ice" in Philadelphia)

For 48 ozs.

4 C water
2 C lemon juice
2 C sugar
one lemon rind, grated or
3 T lemon zest

Boil water and sugar until a syrup forms, then let cool. Add lemon juice and grated rind, along with about 1 lb. (16 oz.) of shaved or flaked ice and stir. One may also add the ice to the syrup and lemon, and then let everything blend, but constantly stir to keep the ice from setting into one piece. Add more ice if preferred to keep the taste light.

Nineteenth century Philadelphians also made ices from raspberries, strawberries, pineapples and other berries sold locally.

THE 7-UP CAKE

The soft drink, 7-Up was formulated by the Imbesi family in South Philadelphia before it became world-known.

3 C cake flour, sifted	1 1/2 C butter or margarine
2 1/2 C sugar	1 C 7-Up
4 eggs	1 t baking powder
zest from one lemon and one lime	

Preheat oven to 325° F and grease and flour a deep cake pan, or 2 cake pans.
Cream sugar and eggs before adding remaining ingredients. Pour into pan(s) and bake for about 1 hour or until inserted knife comes out clean. Ice or sprinkle with 10X sugar.

THE SALOONS'S FROZEN STRAWBERRY MOUSSE
(by Lawrence Irvin, master pastry chef)

1/2 lb. strawberries, fresh or frozen	
1 C 10X powdered sugar	3/4 C water
3/4 C heavy cream	
6 1/2 T granulated sugar	30 ladyfingers (store-bought)

Have some strawberries set aside for garnish. Puree strawberries with 10X sugar in food processor, then pour mix through a sieve. Refrigerate while cooking over medium heat in a saucepan the granulated sugar and water, stirring to a boil for about 3 minutes. Add 3 T of chilled puree and dip each ladyfinger into the syrup. Cut ladyfingers length-wise and line the sides and bottom of a clear, deep bowl. In another bowl with mixer, whip the heavy cream to soft peaks, then fold in remaining strawberry puree mix. Fill a clear bowl lined with the ladyfingers and freeze for about 3 hours. Garnish with the strawberries set aside. Serves 4.

TEA BALLS

1 C butter or margarine
1/2 t vanilla or almond extract
1/2 C crushed walnuts
1/2 C 4X sugar
1 3/4 C flour

Cream butter and sugar, then add remaining ingredients. Roll dough out and make into little balls, about 1" wide. Bake 400°F for about 10 minutes, then roll balls in 4X sugar as a coating. Makes 2-3 dozen.

BENEDETTA GANDOLFO DONATO'S RAILROAD CAKE

1 C sugar
1 1/2 C flour
1 t vanilla
2 eggs, beaten
1 t baking powder
4 T melted butter
1/2 C milk

Mix all ingredients then place in a greased and floured pan to bake at 325°F for about 25 minutes. If this cake is not already sweet enough and too plain, sprinkle with 10X sugar or ice with melted bitter sweet chocolate drippings. It's supposed to look like a "railroad car" when in a loaf pan.

SAMMY CACIA'S COOKIES
(From "Cacia's Italian Bakery")

1 lb. butter
4 eggs
5 1/2 C all-purpose flour
1 1/2 t salt
2 C sugar
4 t vanilla extract
1 t baking soda

Cream butter and sugar in mixer over medium speed then slowly add remaining ingredients. Preheat oven to 375°F and bake cookies that were dropped by spoonful on non-greased pan for 8 to 10 minutes. Sammy said this yields 7 to 9 dozen cookies—he adds chocolate chips to his batch, but nuts, raisins, decorations and icing can be put in and atop these cookies.

JOSEPHINE PARISI'S ST. JOSEPH'S DAY CAKES
A Sicilian Treat!

2 lbs. flour	2 eggs
1 C raisins	2 T sugar (or more)
1 pkg. yeast	1 t vanilla
1-2 C warm water	dash of salt

Soak raisins in warm water and set aside. Dissolve yeast and wait for foaming. Combine all ingredients in large bowl and stir.
Put cooking oil in a skillet and heat over medium heat to fry the batter—make as pancakes, dropping into pan and turning over when edges brown. Remove from pan when done and sprinkle with sugar. To be eaten hot or cold—use these as would crepes!

MARIO LANZA'S MOTHER'S PIZZA di RICOTTA

World-famous tenor Mario Lanza was born in Little Italy and became a "singing actor" in many MGM movies.

Dough:

1 lb. flour	3 T sugar
4 eggs	pinch of salt
3 T peanut oil (vegetable oil)	zest of 1 lemon

Form a soft dough with ingredients and roll out in a large buttered pan that is 3" deep and 10" wide. Next spoon this mixture on top:

5 lbs. ricotta cheese	3 lbs. parmesan or locatelli cheese
16 eggs	5 C sugar
1/2 t nutmeg	juice & zest 1 lemon and 1 orange

Combine cheese, gradually add eggs while stirring, then add sugar and spices with juices and zest. Place on dough, preheat oven to 325°F and bake 2 to 3 hours. Serve like a deep-dish pizza.

CHAPTER 5
SOUTH PHILLY-STYLE ITALIAN

The cuisines from Abruzzo, Naples, Calabria, Puglia and Sicily made a significant impact on Philadelphia's culinary history since immigrants arrived from these areas in the 1880s. Of course, other U.S. cities receiving newcomers from the south central and southern regions produced similar traditional dishes; the recipes here were selected for their difference, yet still are easy to prepare. Macaroni dishes dominated the eating of the poor immigrants of the past, but today the pasta meals are among the most expensive and popular in restaurants who command high prices for what could be made very inexpensively with these recipes.

ALDO LAMBERTI'S AGLIO OLIO

Mr. Lamberti owns 13 restaurants in the Philadelphia area, with "Positano Coast" as his gem in Old City.

1 lb. spaghetti, cooked al dente
3/4 C extra virgin olive oil
1/2 C yellow tomato, diced
salt & pepper to taste
bunch of fresh basil, chopped
1/2 C garlic (or more) chopped
1/2 C red tomato, diced
hot pepper flakes (opt.)

Set aside the prepared, cooked spaghetti. In deep skillet over medium heat, saute garlic in oil until garlic turns golden. Remove from heat and toss in the tomatoes and basil. Season, then pour all and toss with pasta. Serves 4.

RITA SULPIZIO'S "MINIAZ"

1 lb. perciatelli, cooked and drained

6 eggs, beaten with 1 t coarse black pepper

1/2 C locatelli cheese

salt to taste

Mix cooked and drained macaroni together with the wet eggs, then place into a greased cooking pan. Mix in the cheese, season with salt and bake 1/2 hour to one hour at 300°F. When cooled, cut into square pieces. Serves 4.

Another Little Italy "Maccaroni" factory, The "Italian American" stood at 8th & Christian Streets until the 1920s, and competed with its Genovese paesani around the block.

ROSE CALTABIANO GIRARDO'S SEAFOOD LINGUINI

1 1/4 lb. shelled & deveined shrimp, cut into bite-sized pieces
1/2 C olive oil
1/2 C onions. chopped
4 cloves garlic, chopped
1/2 C anchovies, mashed
2 T fresh basil
1/2 T hot pepper flakes
1/2 C white wine
1 lb. scallops
3 1/2 C plum tomatoes
1 1/4 C mushrooms, cut thin
1/4 C capers
1 1/4 lb. linguini, cooked
fresh Italian parsley

Saute onions, garlic, anchovies and basil in oil, then add all seafood and simmer on medium heat until shrimp turn pink. Pour mixture to another pan. In skillet, add tomatoes separately and cook with capers, mushrooms, adding basil and oil as needed for about 15 minutes. Then combine with seafood mix, pour over cooked linguini and serve. Makes 6 servings.

SOUTH PHILLY-STYLE CRABS & SPAGHETTI

Use two(2) crabs per person.
8 cleaned crabs
1 lb. spaghetti
2 cloves garlic, diced
16 oz. prepared tomato sauce
2 T olive oil

Saute garlic in oil, then add crabs and cook until crabs are red. Prepare macaroni as directed. Warm sauce in large pot, then add crabs and simmer on medium heat for about 2 hours. Add the "crab gravy" to the spaghetti and serve.

ITALIAN MARKET FAVORITES

The South 9th Street "Italian Market" arose in the early 20th century from Catharine Street to Federal, on 9th. Philadelphia's City Council had passed a bill allowing for "curb markets" to be placed on the 800 block of Christian Street and South 9th Street, (along with many others throughout the city) on June 11, 1914. The South 9th Street Businessmen's Association was formed as a corporation in April of 1916, after years of trying to prove that a market was necessary in this part of "Little Italy" where southern Italians had been living since the 1890s. In 1908, thousands of eastern Sicilians moved into this neighborhood after a devastating earthquake.

Southern Italians and then eastern Sicilians eventually predominated in the businesses along what was always called "9th Street" to distinguish it from over forty other markets in the city. Since 2000, Mexicans have made their distinctive mark on 9th Street and as of this publication, Mexicans outnumber those of Italian ancestry, doubling the volume of their businesses. As a consequence of the Mexicans at the "Italian Market" the merchants have preferred to use "9th Street" more than "Italian Market" in the public sector. However, the recipes of "9th Streeters" remain as that part of the past when cooking from what was here became as signature dishes from the 19th century immigrants. Here are some:

FRANCES GIUNTA GIORDANO'S EGGS & TOMAT
(From "P. & F. Giordano's Produce")
(Paul Giordano gave this recipe, in memory of his mother.,

12 eggs, beaten
1 clove garlic, diced
"handful of" Italian parsley, chopped
olive or vegetable oil for frying
locatelli (or parmesan) cheese

12 fresh tomatoes, cut small
"lots of onions"
dash of red pepper flakes

basil and oregano

This is a great recipe for use in a cast iron skillet, coated with oil. Saute the garlic and onions, then add the eggs, seasoning and basil. Stir these fast, adding the tomatoes, until it becomes like a "frittat'". Blend like scrambled eggs, or if you make this as an omelet, let it stay with the cheese and cook. Paul Giordano said to keep a loaf of Italian bread on the side to eat with the eggs. This serves 4 to 6.

JOSEPHINE CARDELLI BERNIER'S STUFFED ROAST PORK
(From "Jules' Reliable Meats")

6-8 lb. center cut pork
2-3 roasted peppers (from jar)
1/3 C parmesan cheese, grated
3-4 garlic cloves, diced
1 C spinach

6 slices prosciutto
6 slices soprasotta
1/4 C fresh parsley
2-3 T rosemary
salt & pepper to taste

Butterfly the pork and lay it open to place prosciutto and soprasotta then the peppers, cheese and spinach on top. Some garlic can be put inside—this is optional. Insert pieces of garlic into slits made in pork after it has been rolled up and tied with butcher cord. First brown the pork on high heat in a pan, then place it on an open pan with about 1" water. Sprinkle rosemary, salt and pepper on top and cook in oven set at 325°F for about 1 1/2 hours uncovered, then 2 to 3 hours covered. Smear butter on top to create more browning, if you want. Serves about 6 or more.

Looking northward from South 9th Street at Montrose Street in about 1905, this main thoroughfare, like other wider roadways, was perfect for selling foods and household items. This later became known as the "Italian Market" by 1920. Now it is mostly Mexican.

FRANKIE PERRI'S BROCCOLI RABE CALABRESE

2 lbs broccoli rabe
Blended oil
Hot pepper seeds to taste
3 T garlic, chopped
pinch of salt & pepper to taste

Rinse the broccoli rabe, then cut into pieces. In skillet, heat oil with garlic, then add greens and season. Makes 4 to 6 portions

---

More Italian Market recipes:

CARDULLO'S CHRISTMAS EVE FISH SALAD

1 lb. shrimp, broiled
1 can jumbo lump crabmeat
1 lb. calamari rings, broiled
juice of 3 lemons
salt & pepper
6 lobster tails, broiled
1 clove garlic, diced
1/4 C olive oil
fresh parsley to taste

Broil the seafood before cutting it up and placing it in a bowl. Add the garlic, lemon juice, oil, salt and pepper with the parsley to the fish. Stir together for consistency. Chill before serving. Makes 4 to 6 portions.

FRED MINNITI'S BRACCIOLA

8 oz. (each) flank steak, pounded thin
2 hard boiled eggs, sliced
1 C blended oil to fry
4 oz. ground beef
2 T yellow raisins

Mix ground beef with eggs and raisins together to make stuffing. Heat oil in skillet on medium temp. Stuff each steak, then roll and secure with a toothpick before searing on high heat for about 3 minutes. Discard the oil, keeping rolls in the pan.

Then make this sauce:

1/4 C white wine
4 basil leaves, chopped
1 C tomato sauce (already prepared)
2 T butter
1/4 C ground beef
salt & pepper to taste

Mix ingredients together and add to skillet with meat rolls. Stir. Place skillet into an oven set at 425°F and bake for 12 to 14 minutes until tender. Makes two servings.

MANGIA SUBITO!

(Eat in a hurry!)

or,

WHAT TO DO WITH LEFT-OVER MACARONI

If the macaroni is already in sauce, you can...

- –add a vegetable, like peas

- –add a protein, like tuna or cooked ground meat

- –fry it in a greased pan, then add bits of fresh basil

- –with or without sauce, add any cheese and toss while hot.

MACARONI MORTI

("Dead Macaroni")

or,

WHAT TO DO TO REVIVE LEFT-OVER MACARONI

So you have had macaroni in your refrigerator for how many days...but it still may be good to eat, so...

- –Place it in boiling water to separate pieces, but don't keep it too long in the water

- –or put macaroni in a collander, pour hot water over and loosen pieces

- –or warm the sticky macaroni over a low temperature and add a light cooking oil and stir until loosened

- –steaming the macaroni can also revive it

PAPPARDELLE con PORCHINI
(From "Spasso")

1 lb. pappardelle, cooked and drained
2 fresh porchini mushrooms, in 1/2" pieces
1/2 C sundried tomatoes, in 1/2" pieces
1/4 C brandy "to splash"

3 T olive oil
fresh basil
parmesan cheese on top
1/2 C heavy cream

Put aside the cooked pasta while over medium heat in a skillet carmelize the onion in the oil, then add mushrooms, cream, tomatoes and basil. Season. Stir until consistency before tossing with pasta. Garnish with basil and parmesan. Serves 4.

NEAPOLITAN BOW TIE PASTA WITH VODKA SAUCE
(by "The Philadelphia Macaroni Company")

12 oz. bow tie macaroni
3 garlic cloves, minced
2 shallots, minced
2 T cooking oil
2 t chives

4 C heavy cream
2 C parmesan cheese
3 oz. smoked salmon
2 oz. vodka
2 C white wine

Cook macaroni, drain and set aside. Saute garlic and shallots in oil until golden. Add vodka and wine and simmer over low to medium heat. Add cream, then gradually stir in cheese. Lastly, add salmon and chives. Serves 4.

THE SALOON'S BONASTAI SAUCE
(Use this on any Pasta)

1/2 onion, julienned
1/2 C pancetta, diced
1/2 C white wine
1 sage leaf

2 T extra virgin olive oil
3 porchini mushrooms, thinly sliced
1/4 C marsala wine
1 lg. can (16 oz.) crushed tomatoes

On high heat, saute onion in oil, then stir in pancetta to carmelize. Add sage, mushrooms, wines and cook to boil. Last, add tomatoes and let cook for additional few minutes then stir in any macaroni.

THE SALOON'S PENNE SESSO

1 lb. Italian pork sausage, removed from casing
3 hot peppers, diced in minute pieces
1 medium onion, diced   32 oz. prepared marinara sauce
4 oz. flour   1 lb. cooked penne

Cook and drain penne, setting it aside while making the sauce in a deep pot, simmering all remaining ingredients for 1 hour until sausage is well done. Sauce will boil down and water will evaporate, leaving a thicker sauce. Serve atop prepared penne.

Serves 4.

MR. LUKE MARANO'S PESTO ROTINI SALAD

(Mr. Marano was the former Chair of the National Pasta Association and is owner of The Philadelphia Macaroni Company.)

1 lb. rotini pasta   1 C cherry tomatoes, halved
2 small yellow squash 1/4" thick circles   3 oz. prosciutto, in strips
2 C green beans in 1" pieces   1/2 C toasted walnuts, chopped
1/2 C pesto sauce   1 T red wine vinegar
4 oz. plain yogurt

Cook and drain macaroni. In a large bowl, combine ingredients, then toss with macaroni. Serves 4 hot or cold.

MARY FOTI'S PENNE LISCI con ZUCCHINI
(From "Rosa Foods")

1 lb. penni lisci macaroni   1/4 to 1/2 C Rosa olive oil
2-3 lbs. zucchini, cut in circles   grated parmesan cheese
salt & pepper to taste

Fry zucchini in olive oil until tender. On side, cook and drain penne, then pour zucchini over macaroni. Add cheese and toss. Serves 4.

PENNE a la VINCENT
(This is a recipe La Veranda created for Senator Vincent J. Fumo.)

1 lb. penne, cooked & drained
1/2 C mushrooms, sliced thin
1 lb. plum tomatoes, chopped
1/4 C white wine
2-3 stalks steamed asparagus tips
Parsley
1 lg. can condensed cream
1T garlic
"handful" parmesan cheese
Olive oil
crushed red pepper
salt & pepper to taste

Use about 1/4 C olive oil to saute garlic, then add tomatoes, wine and simmer until tomatoes are soft. Add asparagus tips and mushrooms. Continue to cook for about 5 more minutes. Add cream, cheese and stir. Toss with cooked and drained pasta. Season to taste. Serves 4.

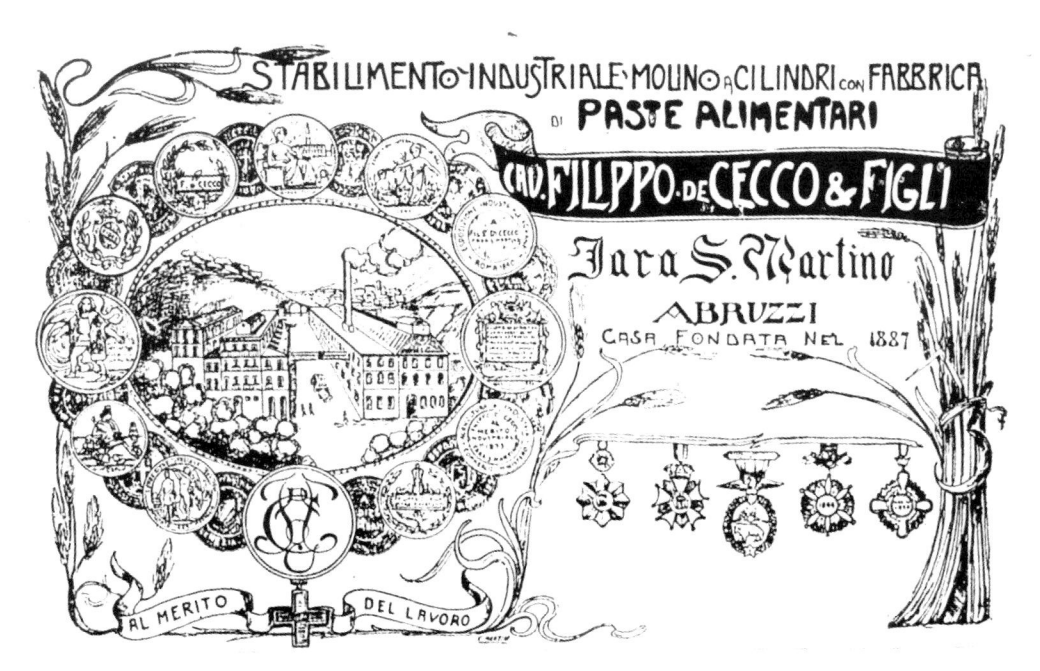

Italian grocers in Philadelphia sold the dry, imported DeCecco pasta in the 1890s when the immigrants had no time to make fresh pasta.

FRANK MUNAFO'S MEDITTERANEAN STEW

1 lb. bass (or scrod or cod)
1/2 lb. Roma (plum) tomatoes
1/4 C parsley, chopped
1/2 C onions, diced
2 T cooking oil
1/2 to 3/4 C white wine

This is so easy! Use fillets. Saute onion in the oil in a deep pan over medium heat. Add parsley, then the tomatoes and white wine. Simmer for a few minutes before adding the fish. Simmer for a few more minutes until fish is tender. When fish is done, drizzle with virgin olive oil on top. Serve with basmati rice. Serves two.

RISTORANTE RADICCHIO'S PORK CUTLETS

2 pork chops, cut 1 1/2" thick
4 T olive oil
1/2 C Spanish onion, chopped
1 sweet red pepper, in strips
1 green pepper, in strips
3 potatoes, par boiled, peeled and cubed
3 cloves garlic
pinch of oregano
bunch parsley
2 T white wine vinegar
8 oz. white wine
salt & pepper to taste

Saute the pork in the oil to brown on both sides, then add the smashed garlic and simmer over medium heat. Add remaining ingredients and cook for 5 minutes. Pour on the wine and place skillet into the oven at 350°F for 10 minutes. Turn off heat and let all remain in the oven for additional 20 to 30 minutes—it'll taste better the longer it stays simmering. Serves about 4.

AUNT EMILIA'S ROASTED CHICKEN & POTATOES

3-4 lb. roaster chicken
Italian parsley, to taste
olive oil
salt & pepper to taste

2 garlic cloves
rosemary to taste
4 to 5 white potatoes, cut
   into quarters

Par boil the potatoes for a few minutes, then drain off the water from the pot. Rinse chicken in salted water, then pat dry. Salt and pepper the chicken's cavity, then insert the garlic, sprigs of parsley and rosemary. Close the cavity and tie legs. One may "grease" the chicken with butter, shortening or oil and salt it before placing the bird in a preheated oven at 350°F for 2 1/2 hours uncovered. After one hour, add the potatoes or other vegetables, that were seasoned and continue baking. Serves about 4.

LOU CARANGI'S TRADITIONAL ITALIAN WHEAT BREAD

12 oz. stone ground wheat flour
1 1/2 oz. sea or Kosher salt
9 oz. water, room temperature

4 oz. cracked wheat flour
2 oz. fresh yeast

Mix all ingredients to rise for 1 1/2 hours, then bake in a preheated oven at 425°F for 20-25 minutes. Makes two loaves.

MICHAEL DiPILLA'S "PASTA a la GRIGLIA"

Make this in a cast iron or aluminum pan with a cover, or use a grill with a lid.

10 round tomatoes
1 lb. dry long ziti
10 fresh basil leaves
salt to taste

1/2 lb. locatelli, grated
1/2 C olive oil
1 C water
ground black pepper (opt.)

Cut tomatoes in quarters and line the entire pan. Hand-break the ziti into 2" lengths, then sprinkle with grated cheese. Pour 1/4 C of the olive oil on top. Lay the basil down on the ziti. Repeat layers. Depending on the pan's size, keep making layers. Pour water over the top–use more if necessary. Then put on the lid and bake on the grill for about one hour covered on low heat, or in an oven over low heat. Serves 4.

JOSEPH DiGIRONIMO'S POLPETTE (Meatballs)
(Director and Lead Chef Instructor at JNA Culinary Institute.)

1/2 lb. each: lean ground beef and lean ground pork
2 t fresh parsley, minced
1/4 C dry breadcrumbs
1 egg, slightly beaten
vegetable or canola oil to fry

2 cloves garlic, crushed
zest of 1 lemon
salt & pepper to taste

Mix ingredients together to a consistency. Take a palm-size amount of meat mix and form a ball. Heat oil in skillet over medium temperature and add meatballs, turning them occasionally for even cooking. When raw meat inside is cooked, meatballs are ready. Depending on size, the yield should be about 10 meatballs.

MARIE URSO'S "MUSSELS IN RED SAUCE"
(From "THE TRIANGLE TAVERN")

24-30 mussels, cleaned and debearded
1/2 lb. linguini, cooked
2 cloves, garlic, diced
1 C parsley
2 C marinara sauce

4 T salt
2 t red pepper flakes
pinch of oregano
4 shots white wine

In a large, deep pot, fill 1/4 to 1/2 with water to cook mussels. Add seasonings and boil on high heat until mussels open. Add the marinara and stir. Lower heat, then serve atop linguini. Serves 2.

CHAPTER 6

"MOB MEALS"

Those of a certain generation seek out the "mob restaurants" when visiting in Philly for Italian food because the guys in the mob know where to eat the best. Here, the price of the food does not dictate the quality, especially in these eateries that were either "owned" by those in the Mafia or were frequented by mobsters in the 1930s to the 1990s. (Our Cosa Nostra Family was imprisoned, causing the "fall" of the Philly Mob.) Having written three books on the history of the Philadelphia Mafia, I got to know many members and their relatives who contributed these recipes. We'll start with the bosses' families:

ROCCO RUGNETTA'S CALAMARI IN TOMATO SAUCE
(From "South Philly Grille")

Rocco's grandfather, Joseph Rugnetta was boss of the local Mafia for a few months in 1958, but he owned the Grille since the 1930s.

- 1 lb. linguini, cooked, on side
- 2 qts. prepared marinara sauce
- 5 lbs. calamari, cleaned–Rocco uses only the tube-like bodies
- 4-5 T salt
- 1/4 C olive oil
- 1 bulb garlic, peeled and chopped
- 2 small onions, diced fine
- 1 T granulated garlic
- basil to taste
- dash of black pepper
- oregano (optional)

Cut the calamari bodies into fours. In a deep pot, boil water and salt. When water boils, throw in calamari for 3 minutes until they start to "curl." Stir as needed. Calamari will turn pink. Strain off water and rinse calamari with cold water.

In another pot, saute garlic first until golden, then add onions. Keep calamari dry on side. Add marinara to garlic and onion mix, season to taste and stir until it boils. Reduce heat then add calamari and stir. Gradually increase heat to a boil for 3 to 4 minutes. Let the pot stand for 5 minutes or more for the calamari to absorb the sauce. The longer the calamari stay in the sauce, the better the taste. Then, serve atop the cooked linguini. Serves 2 to 4 portions.

After boss Angelo Bruno was killed, Philip Testa took over control of the Philadelphia-South Jersey Mob. Testa's family sold poultry on Christian Street since the 1920s, so his parents and siblings knew how to prepare a variety of recipes such as the ones that Philip's sisters Millie (Carmella) and Connie gave to me:

ROASTED CHICKEN a la FAMIGLIA TESTA

6-7 lb. roaster, with skin on
2-3 large white potatoes
2-3 large sweet potatoes
salt, black pepper to taste
1/2 C olive oil
1 peeled lemon or orange
2 onions, sliced in quarters
Italian seasoning and garlic powder to taste

Wash and dry chicken, removing insides. Place chicken in roasting pan after seasoning the entire bird. Stuff the cavity with the lemon or orange. Pour olive oil and 1 C water over the chicken while in the pan. Cover and place in oven preheated at 350°F for one hour, then cook another hour uncovered with the potatoes. When finished, drain liquid and serve. Makes 6 to 8 portions.

CONNIE TESTA'S DELICIOUS CHICKEN

3-4 lbs. chicken wings and legs
2 C bread crumbs (Italian-style)
1 C olive oil

Leave skin on chicken after washing and drying parts. Dip each piece in olive oil, then coat in bread crumbs. Lay on cookie sheet and bake for one hour at 350°F, covered with aluminum foil, then remove foil and bake an additional hour until golden brown, turning pieces during cooking for evenness.

CONNIE TIROTTI BORRIELLO'S PASTA & CECI
Another dish preferred by mobsters, bookies and the guys.

2 T olive oil	1 medium onion, diced
16 oz. can ceci peas	1 lb. elbow macaroni (cooked)
3 cloves garlic, diced	2 T basil
8 oz. can of tomatoe paste and	1 t oregano
8 oz. can stewed tomatoes	salt & pepper to taste

In a large sauce pan heat olive oil and saute garlic and onions. Add tomatoes and stir to boil. Add chickpeas and water, if needed. Cook until everything is consistent–about 10 minutes, then add macaroni and stir together. Serves 4 to 6.

CAVOUR Restaurant
768 So. 8th Street
PER BANCHETTI, SPOSALIZI ecc. visitate il
Sig. GIOVANNI DI LULLO
Eleganti sale rimesse totalmente a nuovo con decorazioni artistiche. Prezzi miti.
Servizio inappuntabile
Tel. WALNUT 9853.

The Cavour Restaurant was one of several successive eateries at this location on South 8th Street, where one had a choice of places to dine among Prohibition gangsters, or not: Eighth Street was a continuous crime scene from the 1920s through the 1950s for local law enforcement.

Mafia boss Angelo Bruno ran Philadelphia from 1959 to 1980 and ate his last meal at Cous' Little Italy Restaurant. Some of Cous' recipes are included in this book, but the "Chicken Sicilian" here was given by Cous to Robert Barretta whose grandfather, Raymond "Long John" Martorano, a mob member, owned Cous' Little Italy.

CHICKEN SICILIAN

4 (8 oz. each) boneless & skinless chicken breasts, cut into 1" cubes and lightly floured

1 whole Spanish onion, sliced	3 T each: blended oil and olive oil
3 cloves garlic, sliced	
16 whole cherry peppers	1 T fresh oregano, basil & parsley
1/2 t kosher salt	
1/2 C Gaeta olives or Sicilians (pitted)	1/2 t coarse black pepper
	1 C white wine
1 stick butter	1 T capers
2 C chicken stock	

In a large skillet, saute chicken in blended oil on medium heat until brown on all sides. Strain oil from pan and add 3 T olive oil, the garlic, onion and saute until golden. When onions are clear, add white wine, peppers, olives and capers. Simmer for about 3 minutes. Add chicken stock and continue to simmer 5 minutes to reduce stock. Roll stick of butter in flour and add to pan, then add fresh herbs last and simmer for 5 minutes more. Sauce will gradually thicken. Serve immediately. Makes about 4 servings.

Another favorite by Cous, made for mobster Frank Sin

FRANK SINDONE SALAD

3 hearts, Romaine lettuce
10 oz. Russian dressing
6 hard-boiled eggs, chopped
1/4 C fresh parsley
1/4 C ketchup

1 head, iceburg lettuce
4 oz. mayonnaise
1 C cooked shrimp, diced
1 t black pepper
salt to taste

Rinse lettuces in cold water, then let dry before refrigerating. In large bowl, whisk mayonnaise, eggs, shrimp and seasonings with Russian dressing and ketchup. Refrigerate for 1/2 hour. Combine chilled lettuce with dressing together. Before serving, garnish salad with any extra hard-boiled egg. Serves 4.

Mafiosi in Philadelphia often used restaurants to discuss their business over food and the Villa di Roma at the Italian Market was one such place that the FBI recorded mobster gatherings in the 1960s and 1970s. Cous Pilla of "Cous' Little Italy" once cooked at the Villa, but now Basil DeLuca is the star chef.

BASIL'S SICILIAN TUNA & PASTA

1 lb. bow tie pasta, cooked
20-24 oz. tuna filets
1 C any vegetable oil to fry
6 black pitted olives
2 cherry peppers with juice
dash of fresh or dried basil

1 (14 oz.) can whole tomatoes
flour to coat filets
1 small onion, diced
4-6 capers
1/2 t garlic powder
salt and pepper to taste

Set cooked macaroni aside. In skillet heat oil for frying. Coat each filet in flour and lay in oiled pan over medium heat. Add onion and saute when onions are done. Drain oil from pan and add tomatoes. Stir and season, add capers, olives and peppers with the juice. Simmer over medium heat for 20-30 minutes until tuna begins to flake into pieces, then spoon atop cooked macaroni. Serves 4.

ROBERT BARRETTA'S PASTA PRIMAVERA

Robert had worked at "Cous' Little Italy," after having worked in New York City's Mulberry Street's eateries.

1 lb. whole wheat fettuccini	6 garlic cloves, thinly sliced
1 T extra virgin olive oil	1 yellow squash, diced
1 small zucchini, diced	1 bag baby spinach (organic)
1 pear-shaped tomato	1 yellow pear tomato
1/2 C Chardonnay	2 C chicken stock

Saute garlic to light color, then add onion and cook for 2-3 minutes. Add other vegetables and continue to stir. Add wine and stock and simmer for about 5 minutes. In another pot, cook macaroni as directed. Drain and add vegetable mix and toss. Top with fresh basil leaves. Serves 4.

Mafiosi settled in the city as well as in suburban Philadelphia. The Mafia is a western Sicilian organization and the cooking in that part of Sicily is different from eastern Sicily and mainland Italy. These recipes are from Palermo and Sciacca in Sicily and they do not have the heavy tomato sauces common to Naples, or the spiciness of Calabrian fare. The dishes are easy and nutritious and I have been eating them all my life, just like my ancestors (although I have been in Philadelphia, relocated from the suburbs.)

MORELLO "NZUOIGGHIU"
(A marinade)

2 cloves garlic, mashed	1/2 C fresh mint, chopped fine
1/2 C extra virgin olive oil	1/2 C wine vinegar or lemon
Lemon	salt & pepper to taste

Use a food processor or mortar & pestle to grind the ingredients together then add the liquids. Stir together for consistency to make a paste. Can be used on meat, fish or potatoes. Use on grill!

ANGELINA'S PASTA chi FINOCCHI SARDE
(Macaroni with fennel and sardines)

This is a signature dish of Palermo.

1 lb. fresh sardines (or canned)	4 T olive oil
4 bulbs fennel with greens	1/2 C golden raisins
1 large onion, chopped	4 cloves garlic, chopped
1/2 C capers	1/2 C Italian breadcrumbs
Salt & pepper to taste	olive oil to fry

In skillet, heat oil over medium heat, then toss in breadcrumbs and stir until toasted. Remove. Add garlic and onions to skillet and saute until golden. On side, chop fennel in fine pieces and add to skillet with onions and garlic. Add 1 C water, seasoning, raisins, capers and sardines then simmer for 1 hour over low heat. Add water if necessary to develop sauce. Pour this atop any pasta that was already cooked and drained. Sprinkle with breadcrumbs and toss. Serves 4 if one pound of pasta is prepared.

PASTA RICOTTA

For 4 servings as main meal.

1 lb. cut macaroni of small or medium size, cooked and drained	1 1/2 lbs. ricotta salt to taste cinnamon (optional)

Cook macaroni as directed and drain, leaving 1/4 cup water. Add ricotta cheese and stir while still hot, melting the cheese. Salt to taste and serve while hot. Sprinkle with cinnamon.

SICILIAN BEEF SALAD

2 lbs. or more, steak, or any cut of cooked beef in 1" pieces	1/2 C celery and celery leaves
	1 C pitted Sicilian olives
	1/2 C onion, diced
1/2 C red wine vinegar	1/4 C extra virgin olive oil
Salt and pepper to taste	

This is a cold salad to make in one bowl by adding all ingredients together the day before eating. Let the beef get marinated well. Makes 6 to 8 servings.

ANCHOVIES & MACARONI

The Philadelphia Italian Market Cookbook originally used spaghetti as the pasta of choice, but a medium-sized cut balances better with the anchovy pieces.

Try to drain oil from canned anchovies.

1 lb. rigatoni, ziti or comparable size macaroni
4 cloves garlic, diced
blended olive oil to fry
salt
1 lb. de-boned anchovies
fresh Italian parsley

Cook macaroni as directed, drain and set aside. In skillet, saute garlic until golden and add anchovies. Stir until anchovies break apart into smaller pieces, then add to macaroni, coating the pasta with the garlic-oil liquid. Add parsley and stir again. Serve with or without grated cheese on top.

ANN'S SEASONED OLIVE OIL

Use this atop meats or fish as a condiment or dressing for flavor.

16-20 oz. blended olive oil
pinch of black pepper
1/2 T each: garlic salt, onion salt and celery seed

Place all ingredients into a flask or bottle and shake to blend.

CHAPTER 7
ONLY ROCKY BALBOA'S PUNCH IS FASTER: PHILLY'S ITALIAN FAST FOODS

Industrial jobs fostered the need to take food with oneself while away from home for long hours. So, when Italian immigrants were recruited to work in the city's manufacturing and production factories, taking a loaf of Italian bread stuffed with meats and vegetables was doable, a very practical way to get nourished. This was not a "Philadelphia" phenomenon, nor an "Italian" concept with the Earl of Sandwich leaving his mark in culinary history. But, regionally throughout the eastern part of the U.S., there began to be "signature sandwiches" that identified the place where the sandwich began a tradition. In Philadelphia's case, the steak sandwich made by homemakers on a grill since the 1700s developed into something a bit different with an Italian influence made popular by Pasquale "Pat" Olivieri in about 1930: since then, the "Philly Steak" or "Philly Cheesesteak" is a must-eat with visitors.

But there were many different types of Italian-inspired sandwiches eaten in Philadelphia before 1930, namely the "hoagie" (or "hoggie" as some old-timers sometimes still call it.) This sandwich is whatever vegetables and proteins get mixed into a long roll with or without olive oil and Italian seasonings. Denise Nanni Campo from "Campo's" often uses this basic recipe.

HOAGIE

2 Italian-style rolls	Italian hams, salamis, etc....
4 Jersey tomatoes	provolone cheese (no other!)
1/4 head iceburg lettuce	extra virgin olive oil
Spanish onion, sliced thin	oregano, salt & pepper to taste

Slice open the rolls, drizzle with oil and add remaining ingredients.

A local tradition in Philadelphia since 1930, "Pat's King of Steaks" relied upon regional Abruzzese cuisine and improved the steak sandwich served at Tun Tavern in the 1700s. "Pat" Olivieri's brother Harry's son Frank and grandson Frank, Jr. have continued making sandwiches that are world-renown.

FRANKIE OLIVIERI'S CAPPELLINI & ASPARAGUS

Frank, Jr. and Frank, Sr. are owners of "Pat's King of Steaks"

1 lb. cappellini, cooked, aside
1 C chicken stock

1/4 C toasted pine nuts
salt & pepper to taste

1/2 lemon, for its juice
1 bunch asparagus in 1/2" pieces
1/2 C pecorino romano cheese

Set cooked pasta aside after draining. In skillet, blanch asparagus in half of chicken stock. Season to taste and simmer for 5 minutes. Add remaining stock and vegetable to pasta and toss with nuts. Squeeze lemon at end, the top with grated cheese before serving. Makes 4 portions.

VONDA BUCCI'S EASTER LAMB & EGGS
(From "John's Roast Pork")

Vonda Bucci is the mother of John who won the James Beard Award.

1/4 C olive oil
1/2 C onion, chopped
3 lb. spring lamb, shoulder cut
1 lg. can chicken broth
8 eggs, beaten

1 stalk celery, chopped
3 cloves garlic, minced
3 dry bay leaves
1/2 t rosemary
1/2 C parmesan cheese

In a Dutch oven, heat oil to saute celery, onion and garlic. Add cubed pieces of lamb, bay leaves, rosemary, salt and pepper. Cook over medium heat for about 10 minutes, stirring. Add broth and simmer for 15 minutes more. When lamb is tender, stir in eggs, stirring slowly so the eggs are scrambled into the broth. Continue to stir until broth is clear and egg is cooked into threads. Spoon this into bowls, sprinkle with parmesan cheese and have some Italian bread on side to soak up the broth. Serves 6 to 8.

NICK'S ROAST BEEF'S LILY'S PASTA & PEAS

Lily is the daughter of Nick DiSipio who founded the sandwich spot.

6 oz. pancetta	1 onion, chopped
3 cloves garlic, chopped	2 lbs. fresh peas
1 t sugar	2 t thyme
3 T extra virgin olive oil	2 heads Boston lettuce
1 lb. spaghetti, cooked on side	parmesan cheese
Salt and pepper to taste	red pepper flakes (opt.)

Saute onion in skillet with oil, then add pancetta and garlic. Add 1/2 C water and simmer, adding peas, sugar and seasonings. Mix leaves of lettuce with skillet blend, then toss with spaghetti. Sprinkle parmesan on last. Serves 4.

TONY LUKE'S "ZITI MICHAEL"
(Yes, THAT Tony Luke!)

1 lb. cooked ziti	1 C veal, in small strips
1 C chicken strips	1/2 C white wine
1/2 stick butter	1 T canola oil
1/2 C flour (to coat)	1/2 t granulated garlic
1/2 t hot pepper flakes	12 oz. marinara sauce, prepared
1 C shredded mozzarella	

Flour year and chicken strips and place in skillet with butter. Add canola oil, season to taste, then add the granulated garlic and hot pepper flakes over medium heat. Add wine and keep cooking until reduced. In a small bowl, make a roux with 1/4 C flour and some drippings, then incorporate into skillet mix, along with the marinara. Lay ziti in a pyrex dish and pour sauce on top. Sprinkle with mozzarella cheese on top and bake in oven set at 450°F for about 5 minutes or until cheese is melted. Serves 4.

ROSINA'S PIZZA
(From "Sarcone's Bakery & Deli")

Luigi Sarcone founded his bakery in 1918; his great-grandson, Lou added a deli up the street from the bakery he also operates. Rosina was Lou's grandmother.

1 prepared pizza shell
3 T olive oil to fry,
more oil to drizzle

4 medium onions, cut in circles
course black pepper

Saute onions in oil with pepper, the spread over raw dough to put into preheated oven at 350°F for 5 to 10 minutes until golden. Drizzle more oil on top after baking. Serves 6 to 8.

An encore from Frankie Olivieri, Jr. who was trained as a chef:

FRANKIE OLIVIERI'S GNOCCHI & CRAB SAUCE
(From "Pat's King of Steaks")

2 T extra virgin olive oil
2 (8 oz.) cans tomatoes
2 C heavy whipping cream

2 cloves garlic, minced
1/2 lb. lump crab meat
1 lb. gnocchi

Cook gnocchi as directed and drain. In skillet, saute garlic in oil, then add tomatoes, cream, crab and season. Stir and cook for about 15 minutes before mixing with gnocchi. Serves 4.

Tony Luke credits "Shank's & Evelyn's" as his inspiration for his many great sandwiches that include a chicken cutlet, roast pork, roast beef and sandwiches packed with vegetables. Pam Perri, the daughter of "Shank" and Evelyn gives this fast recipe where broccoli rabe again is the star ingredient.

PAM PERRI'S RIGATONI & BROCCOLI RABE
(From "Shank's & Evelyn's")

1 lb. rigatoni, cooked
4 C prepared marinara sauce
2 bunches broccoli rabe, diced
salt & pepper to taste
4 cloves garlic, chopped
2 T olive oil
1/2 C water

Cook and drain macaroni and set aside. In skillet, saute garlic in oil over medium heat until golden brown then add broccoli rabe and some water. Season to taste. Let greens simmer until stems are semisoft. Blend in marinara and toss immediately with rigatoni. Serves 4.

Toni Caliva DeRito used to run "The Hungry Hut," but she's now retired and leaves son Pete to run a cart across from Independence Hall, making mostly steak sandwiches for the tourists.

TONI DeRITO'S ITALIAN BEEF SOUP

1/2 lb. or more beef bone
  with chuck on it
4-5 cloves garlic, diced
2 T sugar
1 large can whole tomatoes
salt & pepper to taste
1 C celery
2-3 onions, diced
1 C carrots
2 T basil
1 lb. acini pepe macaroni
  (cooked, on side)

In a large pot filled half with water, add bone with chuck, and let boil with pinch of salt. Wait until beef falls off bone to add remaining ingredients, except for macaroni. Boil until vegetables are done then add macaroni and stir. Add pieces of beef to make the soup fuller, if preferred. Serve with cheese on top. Makes 6 to 8 portions, or more, depending on size of bowl.

9th STREET'S "GEORGE'S ROAST BEEF"

6 lb. eye roast
1 large onion
2-3 cloves garlic
salt & pepper to taste

Preheat oven to 350°F and place roast been in large pan with some water. Cut onion and place at sides. Place pieces of garlic into slits cut into the beef. Season before roasting for 3-4 hours or until beef is tender.

DENISE CAMPO'S LIMA BEANS & PASTA

1 lb. rigatoni
2 cloves garlic, diced
1 can Italian tuna, if in oil, drained
1 small red onion, diced
1 pkg. (1 oz.) lima beans
salt & pepper to taste

Cook rigatoni and set aside. Cook lima beans and place in bowl to mix with tuna, onion, garlic and macaroni. Season to taste. Serve hot or cold. Makes about 4 portions.

"Palumbo's" was so synonymous with Philadelphia's Little Italy that it influenced smaller eateries to emerge in its shadows (literally!) such as "Willie's," "Marie's," "Lorenzo's Pizza," and "Willie's Water Ice" all around Ninth and Christian Streets.

"WILLIE'S SANDWICHES'" TRIPE

Make this with or without tomato, a tradition in Philadelphia.

2 lbs. tripe, cleaned and cut into 1/2" pieces	1-2 C celery, chopped
2 C onions, diced	1 bay leaf
1 T cooking oil	2 T oregano
1 (16 oz. can) tomato puree	salt & pepper

Use more celery and onions if desired to cook tripe with remaining ingredients in deep pot, boiling tripe to tenderness. If using the puree, add the puree while tripe is boiling so tripe will absorb the tomato and have a different taste. Serves 4 to 6 in sandwiches.

CARMEN CURRO'S ITALIAN MEATLOAF
(From "Ricci's Hoagies")

5 lbs ground beef
1/2 lb Maglio's hot Italian sausage, without casing
1 T garlic salt
4 oz. can tomato paste
2 eggs
1/2 C Italian-style bread crumbs
salt and pepper to taste

Mix everything together and bake at 375°F for about 40 minutes.

Maglio's Sausage is served all around Philadelphia and is the choice for using in grilled "Sausage & Pepper" sandwiches or in "Sausage & Gravy" stuffed in Italian steak rolls. Try this dish!

MAGLIO'S SAUSAGES & POTATOES

1 lb. sausage in 1" pieces (preferably sweet Italian)
2 green & 1 red bell peppers
1/2 sprig fresh rosemary
salt & pepper to taste
5 medium potatoes, cubed
2 large Vidalia onions, cut
3 cloves garlic, diced
olive oil

Pan fry sausage in skillet, then set aside. In a pyrex dish with about 1" water, add sausage and remaining ingredients and cover. Bake at 350°F in oven for 1 1/2 hours then remove cover and let potatoes and onions brown on broil for about 10 minutes. Sprinkle top with 1 C Italian seasoned breadcrumbs, if desired. Serves 4.

Marie Masi once owned "Marie's Luncheonette" next to "Palumbo's" where she fed anyone who wanted to "hang out" at her place – a testimony to the atmosphere and food that Marie served. Here's an example of her creativity.

MARIE'S STUFFED ARTICHOKES with SHRIMP

6 artichokes	1 lb. small shrimp
6 cloves garlic, diced	1/2 C grated pecorino romano
1/3 C olive oil	1/4 C Italian parsley
3 C Italian breadcrumbs	chicken broth

Cut stems and bottoms from artichokes, then place each upside down and press to remove leaves. Cut pincers, then rinse artichokes in cold water. Combine in a bowl breadcrumbs, oil and other ingredients and mix to form a soft dough as the stuffing. Fill deep pot with water and add garlic and salt. Add artichokes and cover to boil. Artichokes should be stuffed before boiling; they are done when a leaf is easily removed. Serves 6.

Philadelphia's Reading Terminal Market has several vendors who have their roots in Little Italy and the former Italian Market. They have done well at the Reading Terminal in representing fast food with traditional Italian flair in these recipes.

DOM SPATARO'S TORTELLINI in ALFREDO

(Dom is the owner of "Spataro's" a sandwich shop at the Terminal.)

Alfredo sauce:

1/2 lb. butter (8 oz.)	1/2 lb. reggiano parmesan, grated
1 C heavy cream	1 clove garlic, minced
1/2 t white pepper	

1 lb. tricolor tortellini, cooked and set aside

1 jar roasted red pepper sliced thin	8 oz. broccoli, steamed and set aside
2 T extra virgin olive oil	1/4 t nutmeg (a pinch)
2 cloves garlic	1/2 t white pepper

Cook Alfredo sauce in a deep saucepan over low heat. In skillet, saute garlic in oil and add spinach. Season with nutmeg and the white pepper over low heat. Make a bed with the spinach on a plate and lay the tortellini on top. Pour sauce over and garnish with the roasted peppers and broccoli.

CARMEN DiGULIELMO'S VEAL with CRABMEAT
(From "Carmen's Famous Italian Hoagies")

4 veal cutlets, 1/4" thick and pounded thin
1/4 wedge of lemon
1 lb. lump crabmeat
2 eggs, beaten
2 cloves garlic, diced
2 C good olive oil to fry

1/2 stick butter
1 1/2 C flour
16 asparagus spears
1/2 pint, heavy cream
salt & pepper to taste

Preheat a skillet on medium heat and add oil. Dip cutlets in egg, then coat with flour. Fry until golden brown on both sides. Lower heat and remove cutlets. In same skillet add garlic, cream, butter and lemon juice and stir, making a roux. Add asparagus and simmer for about 10 minutes then remove. Add lump crabmeat into roux and simmer for 4 to 5 minutes, then return veal to mix to infuse flavors. Serves 4.

TOM NICOLOSI'S LENTILS & MACARONI
(From "DiNic's Roast Beef & Pork")

Night before: soak 3/4 lb. lentils in water. Next day, add to lentils in large pot:

5 cloves garlic, chopped, sauteed in
3 T olive oil, with
1 large onion, chopped   3/4 lb. ditalini pasta, cooked

After garlic and onion turn golden, add to lentils with 1 C red wine, 1 C tomato sauce and "pinches" of hot pepper seeds, thyme, oregano, basil, parsley, salt & pepper. Simmer 10-15 minutes, then add pasta and continue to simmer for about 1 hour. Top with cheese and serve. Makes 3 to 4 portions.

AL STARZI'S CHICKEN & SHRIMP WRAPS
(From "Spice Terminal")

(Al had started the "Spice Corner" at the 9th Street Market, then he moved to create "Spice Terminal" at the Reading Terminal.)

1 large chicken breast, in strips – should make 8 strips (2" wide)
8 (10 to 15 ct.) large shrimp   2 cloves garlic, chopped
3 T olive oil   1 C chicken stock
2 plum tomatoes   1/2 C heavy cream
10-12 capers   basil & parsley
salt & pepper to taste

Over medium heat, in the oil, saute garlic. Wrap each piece of chicken around a shrimp and place in skillet, cooking for a few minutes. Drain off oil and add chicken stock and simmer until reduced. Add basil and parsley and season. Cut tomatoes into small pieces and add to stock, then add cream and stir over medium heat until a rose sauce is made, then add capers.

Al uses this to put atop fettuccini, but it can also be an appetizer.

HARRY FINOCCHIO'S VEAL CHOPS with GARLIC SAUCE

Harry was more famously known as "Harry Ochs" from Reading Terminal Market's meat store.

4 veal chops from loin, 3/4" thick and pounded
1/4 C Worchestersire sauce   pinch of nutmeg
2 eggs, beaten   2 C olive oil for frying
2 C Italian bread crumbs

Garlic Sauce:
3-4 cloves garlic, smashed   2 eggs, beaten until thin
salt and pepper to taste

Dredge each chop in eggs with Worchestershire sauce and nutmeg, then coat in breadcrumbs before frying over medium heat in oil. Cook 8 to 9 minutes on each side then place in a baking dish. Set oven for 325°F and make garlic sauce. Pour sauce over chops and bake for 20 minutes in oven to cook sauce. Serves 4.

ROXANNE TRIFILETTI AURIEMMA'S PESTO PIZZA
(From "Claudio's King of Cheese")

1 round pizza shell, or prepared dough to fit a 10" square pan
1 1/2 pint pesto sauce   1 C extra virgin olive oil
1 large ball mozzarella, shredded

Oil the pizza pans to use with the round shell or prepared dough. Lay doughs and shell down to fit, then spoon the pesto atop the dough. Liberally drizzle some oil on top pesto, then toss cheese on top. Bake in preheated oven set at 325°F until dough is golden or browned to one's liking: Watch pizza cook to prevent burning.

HENRY GEORGE'S CALABRESE SALAD
(From "Chickie's Italian Deli")

(Henry has won so many "Best of Philly" Awards, beginning with his famous vegetarian sandwiches.)

5 romaine lettuce leaves	1/4 head, iceberg lettuce
1 (6 oz.) can Italian tuna	1/4 of an onion, chopped
2 wedges, tomato	3 pieces red bell pepper
6 black oil-cured olives, pitted	1 hard-boiled egg, halved

Arrange all ingredients on plate, then separately mix the dressing in a flask or cup.

This is a colorful salad!

Henry's "House Dressing":

3 cloves garlic, chopped fine	pinch red pepper seed
1/4 C balsamic vinegar or red wine vinegar	1 C olive oil (not extra virgin) oregano, salt & pepper to taste

DOLORES ALVINI'S NEAPOLITAN BEAN SALAD
(From "Willie's Water Ice")

1 (16 oz. can) black beans
1 (16 oz. can) red kidney beans
1 (16 oz. can) ceci peas
1/2 C red pepper, diced small
1/4 C olive oil
2 C each: red onions and celery
1/3 C red wine vinegar
salt & pepper to taste

Rinse beans through cold water to remove starch. (Do this in a colander.) Place beans in a large bowl with rest of ingredients, adding oil, vinegar and seasonings last. Toss and refrigerate. Serves about 8.

DAN'S STUFFED BREAD
(From "Vilotti & Pisanelli Bakery")

Dan was once the owner of the bakery–he served "Pat's Steaks," "Geno's Steaks" and others, making the long "Italian roll."

1 large loaf of "fat" Italian bread that's 12-18" long

1/2 lb. sliced pepperoni
1/2 lb. sausage bits, cooked and diced
2 to 3 hard boiled eggs, cut up
1/4 lb. each: sliced mozzarella, provolone and capicola

Cut loaf horizontally leaving about 1/4 of the top off. Scoop out the bread's insides and line the bottom and sides with the meats, cheeses and egg pieces. Wrap the loaf in aluminum foil and bake low at about 250°F for about 15 minutes or until all cheeses melt. Serves about 6.

SAM AGRESTA'S ANTIPASTO
(From "Sammy's")

Sam used to have his shop in-between "Pat's" and "Geno's" and he did well in business without selling steaks!

The day before, combine these ingredients:

1 (#10) can artichokes, cut in half	1 clove garlic, chopped
1 t salt and pinch pepper	4 oz. olive oil
2 t garlic powder	4 oz. red wine vinegar (or more)

Let everything marinate overnight.

The next day, in a large dish, arrange artichoke mix with:

6 or more roasted peppers	1/2 lb. cubed sharp provolone
1 C marinated mushrooms	1 C each: black & green olives
1/2 lb. each: sliced soprasata and prosciutto	

Sam suggested to be creative with the ingredients – make the dish look good with the colors and shapes. Serves 6 or more.

Joey Vento, owner of "Geno's Steaks" told me that he really doesn't cook, but he did give this tidbit on what makes Philly steak sandwiches so good: it's in the cooking oil. Some steak shops use cottonseed oil, while others blend their own spices and add them to their oils when they cook up the steaks on the grills. Onions also absorb the herbs and spices. Here are some oils to make:

ROSEMARY-FLAVORED OLIVE OIL

16-20 oz. blended olive oil
pinch of salt & pepper

6" sprig of fresh rosemary
or 3 T dried

Blended olive oil is recommended for cooking because it won't evaporate in the heat as fast as extra virgin olive oil.

Combine all ingredients into a flask or empty bottle and let fuse together at room temperature for a few days before using.

BASIL-FLAVORED OLIVE OIL

16-20 oz. blended olive oil
pinch of salt & pepper

4 whole fresh basil leaves

Directions as above with the rosemary.

How to use these olive oils:

To fry vegetables, fish, meats or other foods in skillet; or,

Pour these oils atop vegetables, fish and meats before broiling or baking, whether in an oven or over a grill.

Then, while cooled, use this vinaigrette:

VINAIGRETTE

Some people use a 2:1 ratio of vinegar to oil, or a 3:1 to taste.

1/2 C extra virgin olive oil	1 C red wine vinegar
2 cloves garlic, smashed	1/2 T oregano
salt & pepper to taste	1/2 T sugar (white, granulated)

Mix together and pour atop foods. Refrigerate after use.

SALADS

Left-over vegetables and meats make nutritious salads as entrees or sides. Leave the foods cold and toss with an extra virgin olive oil and vinegar, or just use a good balsamic vinegar, salt and pepper and eat. Here are some suggestions:

Cut cold baked potatoes in quarters, add fresh Italian parsley, 1/4 C roasted red pepper in small pieces and a pinch of chives. Leave skins on potatoes for the texture.

Cube cold chicken breast, without skin for 1 C portion. Add 1/4 C red onion, chopped, 1 orange in halved segments, 1/4 C walnuts, finely chopped and drizzle with balsamic. Serve atop fresh spinach.

Halve one cup of green olives (use only brine-soaked), add one cup of ceci beans (rinsed), 1/2 roasted red pepper, in small pieces, 1/4 C pine nuts, chopped, and pinch of thyme and pinch of rosemary. Use oil-vinegar mix and serve next day after refrigerating overnight.

Use 1 C leftover beef roast or steak or any beef already cooked and cold to add to 1/4 C sweet onion, chopped, pinch of garlic salt, 1/2 to 3/4 C fresh spinach, chopped and mixed with viniagrette. Marinade for 2 hours then serve atop cold rice or between slices of bread.

Angelo Caranco's Beer Saloon, shown here in about 1910 served locally-made Schmidt's along with wines and liqueurs.

The "small bites" at the bar were mainly hard-boiled eggs, salted for more thirst.

Italians have a toast: "Cent'anni!" meaning in one word to wish someone "One Hundred Years!"

The recipes in this cookbook are a guarantee to good cooking and good health by eating what lovers of Italian food have been doing in Philadelphia for 300 years!

A pushcart vendor at 7th and Catharine Streets in 1911 offered his wares near Casa Ravello (a social welfare center) and The House of Industry, both immigrant havens in Philadelphia's Little Italy. (Source: Temple University Urban Archives)

RECIPE INDEX

APPETIZERS

Claire DiLullo Schiavone's "Moonstruck" Pepper-Anchovy Appetizer, 2

Al Starzi's Chicken & Shrimp Wraps, 78

Sam Agresta's Antipasto, 81

Connie Testa's Chicken Wings, 60

BEEF & VEAL

"Mama Yolanda's" Liver Casalinga, 5

Martina Giunta's Veal Roast, 8

Bonzetta (Stuffed Veal), 17

"Scannicchio's" Veal Milanese, 18

"Marra's" Veal Florentine, 19

Bishop James Schad's Skirt Steak, 25

"D'Medici's" Stuffed Steak, 29

Fred Minniti's Bracciola, 51

Joe DiGironimo's Meatballs, 58

Sicilian Beef Salad, 65

"George's" Roast Beef, 73

"Willie's" Tripe, 74

"Ricci's Hoagies" Meatloaf, 75

"Carmen's Famous Hoagies" Veal & Crab, 77

"Harry Ochs" Veal Chops, 78

BREAD & PIZZA

Lou Carangi's Italian Wheat Bread, 57

Rosina Sarcone's Onion Pizza, 71

Roxanne Auriemma's Pesto Pizza, 79

Dan Pisanelli's Stuffed Bread, 80

FILLINGS

South Philly-Style Cheese filling, 14

Ligurian-Style Ravioli/Lasagna filling, 28

MACARONI/ PASTA

Lynn Rinaldi's Pappardelle con Funghi Ragu, 2

Fresca Pasta Lombarda, 16

"La Buca's" Gnocchi a la Fiorentine, 18

Marie Miglino's Ricotta Gnocchi, 19

"Bistro Romano's" Macaroni & Beans, 30

Aldo Lamberti's Aglio Olio, 45

Rita Sulpizio's Miniaz', 46

"Spasso's" Pappardelle con Porchini, 53

Bow Ties in Vodka Sauce, 53

"Rosa Foods'" Penne with Zucchini, 54

"La Veranda's" Penne a la Vincent, 55

Michael DiPilla's Pasta on the Grill, 57

Recipe Index

Connie Borriello's Pasta & Ceci, 61

Basil DeLuca's Sicilian Tuna & Pasta, 63

Robert Barretta's Pasta Primavera, 64

Angelina's Pasta with Sardines & Fenne, 65

Pasta Ricotta, 65

Frank Olivieri's Cappellini & Asparagus, 69

"Nick's Roast Beef's" Pasta & Peas, 70

"Tony Luke's" Ziti Michael, 70

Pam Perri's Rigatoni & Braccoli Rabe, 72

Dom Spataro's Tortellini Alfredo, 76

"DiNic's" Macaroni & Lentils, 77

OILS, VINEGARS & MARINADES

Flavored Vinegar, 6

Mrs. Marano's Italian Salad Dressing, 10

Morello 'nzuoigghiu (marinade), 64

Ann's Seasoned Olive Oil, 66

Rosemary-Flavored Olive Oil, 82

Basil-Flavored Olive Oil, 82

Vinaigrette, 83

Henry George's House Dressing, 79

OTHER MEATS

Roasted Lamb, 9

"Il Portico's" Rice with Quail, 31

Vonda Bucci's Easter Lamb & Eggs, 69

PORK	Italian Sausage, Peppers & Onions, 9
	Sausage & Broccoli Rabe, 17
	Cardelli's Stuffed Roast Pork, 49
	"The Saloon's" Penne Sesso, 54
	"Radicchio's" Pork Cutlets, 56
	The Philadelphia Hoagie, 68
	"Maglio's" Sausage & Potatoes, 75
POULTRY	"La Locanda del Giottone's" Italian Duck, 4
	Chicken Livers from "Villa di Roma Restaurant", 7
	Marion Caltabiano's Turkey Scallopini, 12
	Kippee Palumbo's Rosemary Chicken (or Turkey), 12
	Aunt Emilia's Roasted Chicken Abruzzese, 57
	Cous' Chicken Sicilian, 62
	The Testa Family's Chicken with Orange, 60
SALADS	"Melograno Ristorante" Insalata, 3
	"Scannicchio's" Frank Sinatra Salad, 18
	Sicilian Blood Orange Salad, 22
	Jim Trovarello's Seafood Salad, 22
	Pesto Rotini Salad, 54
	Cous' Frank Sindone Salad, 63
	"Chickie's" Calabrese Salad, 79
	Dolores Alvini's Neapolitan Bean Salad, 80
	Four salads from left-overs, 83

Recipe Index

SAUCES ("GRAVIES")
- "The Saloon's" Livornaise Sauce, 17
- "Ristorante Illuminare's" Pesto Sauce, 26
- Traditional Pesto Sauce, 26
- Caper Sauce, 26
- "The Victor Cafe's" Bechamel Sauce, 28
- Mrs. Auriemma's Basic Tomato Sauce, 32
- "The Saloon's" Putanesca Sauce, 32
- "Shank & Evelyn's" "South Philly Gravy", 33
- Miglino's Marinara Napolitana, 33
- Jim Campenella's Pomodoro Sauce, 33
- "Palumbo's Nostalgia's" Bolognese Sauce, 34
- "The Saloon's" Bonastai Sauce, 53
- "Harry Och's" Garlic Sauce, 78

SEAFOOD
- Aunt Connie Ippolito's Mussels in White Sauce, 3
- Little Italy Tuna, 5
- Antonetta Caruso Marano's Breakfast Flounder, 6
- Steve Candeloro's Honey Salmon, 8
- Marco Avigo's Risotto Lombarda, 16
- "Palumbo's" Crab Cakes, 20
- "Dante & Luigi's" Clams & Spaghetti, 21
- Fish & Lemons, 23
- Mussels Genovese, 27
- "La Buca's" Shrimp & Beans, 29
- "La Veranda's" Pompano, 30
- Rose C. Girardo's Seafood Linguini, 47
- South Philly Crabs & Spaghetti, 47
- Cardullo's Fish Salad, 51
- Frank Munafo's Mediterranean Stew, 56
- "The Triangle Cafe's" Mussels in Red Sauce, 58
- "South Philly Grille's" Calamari, 59
- Anchovies & Macaroni, 66
- Frank Olivieri's Gnocchi & Crab Sauce, 71
- Marie's Stuffed Artichokes with Shrimp, 76

Philadelphia Cooks Italian

SOUPS	"DiNardo's Famous Crabs'" Crab Soup, 22

Toni DeRito's Italian Beef Soup, 72

SWEETS	"Bistro Romano's" Tiramisu, 35

Pietro D'Abbraccio's Coffee Gelato, 36

Buddy Cianfrani's Cup Custard, 36

"D'Orazio Foods'" Ricotta Pie, 37

"Ernesto's 1521 Cafe's" Mugliaccio Pudding, 37

Joe DiGironimo's Panna Cotta, 38

Lou Carangi's Italian Raisin Bread, 38

Dr. LoBianco's Italian Cream filling, 39

Basic Italian Cookie Dough, 40

La Terza Family's Italian Wedding Cookies, 40

Italian Sponge Cake, 41

Aunt Stella's Ricotta Cake, 41

Italian Lemon Ice, 41

7-Up Cake, 42

"The Saloon's" Strawberry Mousse, 42

Tea Balls, 43

Benedetta Donato's Railroad Cake, 43

Sammy Cacia's Chocolate Chip Cookies, 43

Josephine Parisi's St. Joseph Day Cakes, 44

Mario Lanza's Mother's Pzza di Ricotta, 44

Recipe Index

VEGETABLES

Annamarie Michetti's Wild Rice Salad, 5

Barbara Moses' String Bean Side, 7

Mushroom side, 9

Fava Bean Patties, 10

Lentils, Roman-Style, 10

Escarole & White Beans, 13

Broccoli & Macaroni, 13

Cauliflower Parmesan, 13

Parmesan Beans, 14

Spalagi a la Salvatrice (Asparagus), 14

The La Terza's "Jumbot", 20

Vegetable Medley, 30

"P. & F. Giordano's" Eggs & Tomatoes, 49

Frankie Perri's Broccoli Rabe Calabrese, 51

Denise Campo's Lima Beans & Pasta, 73

"Cook's Notes"